the SEWING BIBLE
CLOTHING

WENDY GARDINER

the SEWING BIBLE
CLOTHING

WENDY GARDINER

D&C

David and Charles

www.rucraft.co.uk

David & Charles is an F+W Media Inc. company
4700 East Galbraith Road, Cincinnati, OH 45236

First published in the UK and US in 2010

A catalogue record for this book is available from the British Library.

ISBN-13: 978-0-7153-3765-3 paperback
ISBN-10: 0-7153-3765-3 paperback

Printed in China by RR Donnelley
for David & Charles
Brunel House, Newton Abbot, Devon

Publisher Alison Myer
Acquisitions Editor Jennifer Fox-Proverbs
Editor James Brooks
Project Editor Karen Hemingway
Art Editor Charly Bailey
Photographer Lorna Yabsley
Illustrators Ethan Danielson and Samantha Elliott
Production Controller Kelly Smith
Pre Press Jodie Culpin

David & Charles publish high quality books on a wide range of subjects.
For more great book ideas visit: **www.rucraft.co.uk**

CONTENTS

INTRODUCTION

WELCOME TO MAKING YOUR OWN CLOTHING.
WHETHER YOU ARE A NEWBIE OR AN EXPERIENCED
SEAMSTER, THIS BOOK AIMS TO BECOME YOUR
SEWING COMPANION NO MATTER WHAT
DRESSMAKING PROJECT YOU WISH TO TACKLE.

YOU WILL FIND CLEAR GUIDANCE ON THE TOOLS
AND EQUIPMENT THAT MAKE SEWING SO MUCH
EASIER NOWADAYS, FOLLOWED BY ALL THE BASIC
SEWING SKILLS YOU NEED TO GET STARTED, AN
IN-DEPTH LOOK AT COMMERCIAL PATTERNS
AND ADVICE ON HOW TO MAKE THE RIGHT
FABRIC CHOICES.

THERE ARE FIVE CHAPTERS THAT FOCUS ON
DIFFERENT ESSENTIAL GARMENTS TO HELP YOU MAKE
YOUR OWN CAPSULE WARDROBE — FROM SKIRTS,
THROUGH DRESSES, TROUSERS, TOPS AND BLOUSES, TO
TAILORED JACKETS AND COATS — EACH WITH A
SELECTION OF TOP 10 SEDUCTIVE STYLES TO CHOOSE
FROM. SKIRTS ARE USUALLY EASY TO MAKE, WHEREAS
JACKETS AND COATS REQUIRE A LITTLE MORE
KNOWLEDGE AND PRACTICE, BUT NONE IS TOO
DIFFICULT BECAUSE ALL THE TECHNIQUES YOU WILL
TYPICALLY NEED FOR EACH TYPE OF GARMENT ARE
CLEARLY EXPLAINED. SO YOU CAN EASILY ADD TO

YOUR SEWING REPERTOIRE. EACH GARMENT TYPE IS BROUGHT TO LIFE BY ONE OR TWO PHOTOGRAPHED MODELS AND IN EACH CHAPTER YOU WILL ALSO FIND EXPERT TIPS AND SEWING SUGGESTIONS THAT HELP MAKE DRESSMAKING EASIER, ENSURING PROFESSIONAL RESULTS EVERY TIME.

GO ON — ARM YOURSELF WITH THE KNOWLEDGE TO SEW WITH CONFIDENCE AND PRODUCE GARMENTS WITH DEFINITE 'WOW' FACTOR!

TOOLS AND EQUIPMENT

HAVING THE RIGHT TOOLS FOR THE JOB CAN MAKE SO MUCH DIFFERENCE BOTH TO THE EASE OF CONSTRUCTING GARMENTS AND TO THE FINISHED RESULTS. THIS CHAPTER EXPLAINS WHICH TOOLS ARE ESSENTIAL FOR ACHIEVING AN ACCURATE AND PROFESSIONAL FINISH, AND WHICH TO PUT ON YOUR 'WISH LIST' FOR MAKING LIFE SO MUCH EASIER!

MEASURING AND MARKING TOOLS

The first step in dressmaking is measuring and marking special features. Once a pattern is cut out, you then transfer any markings for pockets, pleats, darts and buttons from the tissue to the fabric. Traditional tailor's tacks can be used, but other quicker methods work as well. With all the following tools, it is advisable to mark on the reverse of fabric.

TAPE MEASURE

It's essential to have a good tape measure. If you have had one lurking around for years, ditch it now – old tapes stretch and so can be inaccurate. A new retractable tape measure, preferably with metric and imperial measurements, is ideal.

CHALK MARKERS

A chalk marker is probably the quickest method of marking the fabric and is easily brushed away once used. Chalk markers come in a variety of shapes and colours, from simple blocks of chalk with shaped edges to chalk wheels and pencils. It's a good idea to have a selection handy.

Chalk pencils come in different colours so you can choose one to show up on the colour of the fabric or to colour code the type of marking. Some have plastic brushes at the end to help brush away the chalk once the markings have been used.

A chalk wheel has a serrated roller and loose chalk encased in a plastic housing. The wheel is rolled along the placement lines for darts, pockets, pleats, hems, etc. and leaves a trail of fine chalk dust. Wheels are simple to use, but may work in one direction only.

Chalk triangles/blocks also come in different colours. They leave a heavier chalk line than the wheel, but can be used in any direction.

MARKER PENS

As pens are very quick to use, they are also handy to have in the workbox. There are different types available from permanent marker pens to vanishing and water-soluble varieties.

> ### SEWING SENSE
> *Check whether the pen markings 'bleed', disappear or stay visible on fabric scraps before committing to marking the fabric for the actual garment.*

Vanishing pens are also called fade-away or air-soluble pens. The marks disappear after a limited time period – usually between 24–48 hours. So you need to be sure that you are going to finish your sewing relatively quickly.

Water-soluble pens disappear when dampened with water, so you can sponge them away or wash them away when laundering the garment.

CARBON PAPER

Another traditional method of transferring markings, carbon paper comes in packs of different light and dark colours. It is used in conjunction with a tracing wheel. The carbon is placed, faced down on the wrong side of fabric with the tissue on top. The placement markings are transferred by rolling the tracing wheel along the appropriate lines on the tissue. You can mark two layers of fabric at a time by placing two pieces of carbon paper, one on top of each layer, or a folded piece of carbon paper between the layers. However, remember to mark the wrong side of the fabric as these marks are permanent; you may need to refold the fabric pieces so that wrong sides are together before marking.

> ### SEWING SENSE
> *Remove any markings before pressing the fabric with a hot iron as the heat can permanently set in even vanishing markings.*

CUTTING TOOLS

SEWING SENSE
Keep dressmaking shears just for dressmaking and away from the rest of the household! Tiny nicks in the blades, caused by cutting household objects, can snag fabric easily. Scissors also blunt quickly when used to cut paper.

Embroidery/needlework scissors are small and sharp with pointed blades, so are very useful for snipping into small areas close to the stitching, around corners and notches, and when clipping and notching seams (see p. 26). Some embroidery scissors have a curved tip, which is particularly handy for cutting thread ends very close to the fabric.

Pinking shears have serrated edges on the blades, which produce a zigzag cut that helps to prevent fabric fraying. Like dressmaking shears, they also have shaped handles. They work best on cottons, craft fabrics, felt, etc. and are useful for neatening raw edges quickly.

General-purpose scissors are useful for cutting everything else, such as templates, cardboard, pattern tissue. The handles are generally the same so they can be used left- or right-handed. Some scissors have soft, padded handles, which make repeated cutting easier on the hand.

SHEARS AND SCISSORS

The most obvious cutting tool is a pair of scissors, but for dressmaking, the blades need to be very sharp and in good condition. The ideal set would include dressmaking shears, embroidery scissors, pinking shears, and general-purpose scissors for cutting paper patterns.

Dressmaking shears have contoured handles with a larger aperture for fingers and a smaller one for the thumb. Right- and left-handed versions are available as it is very uncomfortable to use shears in the wrong hand. The blades are long and straight so you can take long smooth cuts. Sometimes the handles are angled from the blades to make them easier to hold with the blades parallel to the cutting edge, keeping the fabric flat. Others have very tiny serrated edges to gently grip the fabric as it is cut. This is particularly useful when working with slippery fabrics such as silk, organza and chiffon.

OTHER USEFUL CUTTING TOOLS

A **seam ripper**, also known as a quick-unpick, is a nifty device, which comes as a standard tool with most sewing machines. However, over time they do blunt with use, so replace them occasionally. The ripper has a curved blade with a pointed end that can be slipped through unwanted stitches to cut the threads. You do need to use them with care, so that they don't also rip through fabric unexpectedly.

EXPERT TIP
Use a quick-unpick to cut open a buttonhole. Place a pin at one end fractionally before the end of the buttonhole and then from the other end, push the blade between the rows of buttonhole stitches towards the pin.

Rotary cutters come in a range of sizes and with different blades to produce straight cuts or fluted edges. They have to be used in conjunction with a cutting mat as they can slice through several layers of fabric at a time. Some brands have retractable blades and interchangeable heads to provide different cutting options to suit the project. They are ideal for cutting fabric strips for bias binding and for patchwork and quilting. They need storing with care so that the blade can do no damage.

PINS AND WEIGHTS

Pins are used to temporarily hold fabric layers together before they are basted or sewn. Over time they will blunt with use so replace them regularly to avoid them snagging fabric. There are different types of pins, suitable for different purposes such as dressmaking, quilting, lace-making and upholstery. Dressmaking pins are made from tempered hardened steel and can be short and steel-headed or longer, in different thicknesses, with glass or plastic heads.

> ### SEWING SENSE
> *Glass or plastic-headed pins are easier to remove and see if dropped on the ground. However, beware when pressing as plastic heads can melt!*

If working with fabric that can't be pinned or may be damaged by pinholes, use weights (or tin cans) to hold the layers together as you cut. These are particularly useful when working with suede, leather and furs. Once cut out, use double-sided basting tape to hold the seams together before stitching or hold them in place with bulldog clips that don't pierce the fabric.

NEEDLES

Different needles are available for sewing different fabrics. They need to be replaced regularly as blunt ones can cause all sorts of problems, from snagging fabric to skipped stitches. The most common and useful machine needles are listed on p. 12, but you will also need the hand sewing needles below.

HAND NEEDLES

Hand needles are an essential component of any sewing kit and should include a good selection for a wide range of hand-sewing tasks, including slip stitching, hemming by hand, sewing on buttons and beading, etc.

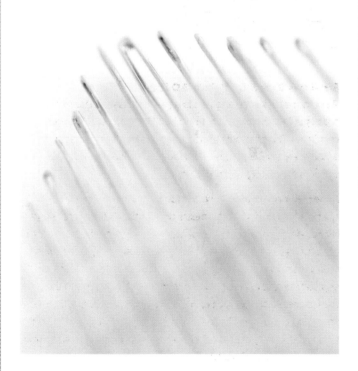

Mixed household needles are useful for hemming, repairing, button sewing, etc. A mixed pack provides a selection of needles with different sized eyes, thicknesses and lengths of shaft, so something suitable for most household jobs.

SEWING SENSE

Self-threading needles have an innovative design with a split eye at the top through which the thread is slotted easily. They are great for those with difficulty seeing the needle eye.

Beading needles are extremely thin with very small eyes so they can slip through the holes in tiny seed beads. They can be straight or curved.

Bodkins are used to thread elastic or cord through casings. Not a needle as such but similar in shape, bodkins have a thicker shaft, a large eye and sometimes a bobble at each end to make it easier to push through casings without catching the tip.

MACHINE NEEDLES

Sewing machine needles have a flat surface on one side of the shaft to ensure correct insertion into the needle holder. Usually this is placed towards the back of the holder (flat to back), but it's wise to check your user manual. If inserted incorrectly, the needle may work loose, stitches can be missed or thread broken.

SEWING SENSE

The higher the number on the needle, the larger and stronger it is.

SEWING SENSE

Insert the needle as far into the holder as possible. Tighten the retaining screw first by hand and then using the screwdriver provided. Failure to tighten it fully can result in the needle working loose, moving about and hitting the throat plate, or dropping out.

Sewing machine needles come in a range of types and sizes to suit different fabric types and weights. Choose the correct needle for the purpose to avoid broken or skipped stitches. Packs are usually numbered with both American (9–20) and European (60–120) sizes. A needle that's too big can leave holes, pucker seams or break threads. If the stitches break and skip, the needle may be too small, so try a larger size. Also, use a larger size needle than you would normally for a particular fabric if you are stitching through lots of layers.

US SIZE	EU SIZE	FABRICS
9–11	60–75	lightweight, sheer or fine fabrics, e.g. lingerie, silk, chiffon, voile, organza, georgette
12	80	general dressmaking, lightweight cotton, silk, satin, polyester, velvet
14	90	medium-weight dressmaking fabrics: polyester, wool, cotton blends, corduroy, fleece
16–18	100–110	heavyweight fabrics, e.g. dense denim, canvas, coating, wool tweed, heavy brocade
20	120	thick and coarse heavyweight fabrics, e.g. upholstery fabric

General-purpose universal needles are suitable for most woven fabrics. Universal needles have a sharp point and come in a range of sizes.

Ballpoint/stretch needles have a rounded tip that parts the fabric fibres rather than pierces them. Use them when sewing stretch fabrics, fleece or velvet. They may have a 'scarf' on the shaft to help part two-way stretch fabrics such as Lycra® and lingerie and rubberized fabrics.

Microfibre/sharps needles are very fine and used for sewing fine, densely woven fabrics such as silk.

Jeans needles are heavier weight and robust, suitable for sewing thick dense fabrics such as denim, upholstery fabrics, faux suede or for top stitching with thicker threads.

Metallic needles have a specially coated eye to help prevent metallic threads shredding, which can happen with a general-purpose needle. (Metallic threads can also wear a tiny groove in the eye of a general-purpose needle, which will then catch the thread as it runs through, causing skipped, broken or missed stitches).

Twin needles have two needles on one shaft and can be used on nearly all sewing machines. They allow you to stitch two perfectly parallel rows of stitching at the same time. Underneath, the bobbin thread zigzags between the two top threads. You can get universal, embroidery and ballpoint twin needles with varying distances between the needles.

SEWING SENSE

Replace the machine needle after every sewing project or eight hours of sewing.

THREADS

Gone are the days when you buy a reel or two of cotton – for whatever you are sewing. Nowadays there are many types of thread to suit a wide range of fabrics and applications. Generally speaking it is a good idea to sew like with like, so cotton fabrics with cotton threads and silks with silk threads. Buy two reels per project and, unless using specialist threads, use the same in top and bobbin. Branded threads are a better buy as they are spun in whole lengths, whereas some cheap threads will be spun from short lengths woven together, making them more liable to break and shred.

SEWING SENSE

Colour match thread as closely as possible to the fabric. If a perfect match is not possible, choose a thread slightly darker as it will appear lighter once it comes off the reel.

General-purpose threads are usually polyester-covered cottons, which combine the strength of cotton with the flexibility of polyester. This makes them suitable for most sewing projects.

Topstitch/buttonhole thread is thicker as it is meant to be visible. Use it for top stitching, making buttonholes, decorative stitching, etc. Use it with a jeans or embroidery needle, both of which have larger eyes, with a general-purpose thread in the bobbin.

Metallic threads are speciality threads used to add glitter and sparkle when top stitching or to add surface interest with decorative stitches. Use a metallic needle.

EXPERT TIP

If a thread is thick or knobbly, wind it onto the bobbin by hand, with a general-purpose thread in the top, and then sew with the project face down.

Quilting threads have a wax finish, which helps prevent them from tangling. They can be used for machine or hand stitching.

Basting thread is finer and rougher than general-purpose thread and usually 100% cotton. It is used to temporarily hold layers together so it breaks easily.

Invisible thread can be clear or smoke-coloured. It is made from nylon and designed for invisibly attaching trims. It can also be used for quilting or repairs.

Machine embroidery threads are finer than general-purpose threads and are thus suitable for high density stitching, not general seaming. They are good for decorative and top stitching. Types include metallics, variegated and iridescent. They are usually made from rayon and have a high sheen. Use them with a machine embroidery needle.

Bobbinfil is a very fine thread in white or black, designed to work with embroidery threads. Its weight minimizes the bulk of thread on the underside of dense machine embroidery designs, which helps prevent puckering.

Serger threads are finer than machine sewing threads or have a woolly appearance, which is softer against the skin. A serger (overlocker) uses far more thread for every seam than a sewing machine as it sews two straight rows and encases the raw edges with thread. Therefore serger threads come in larger quantities on cones or cops (also known as bobbins). Use 100% polyester or cotton-wrapped polyester in the needles. For the loopers, you can use the same thread or woolly nylon/floss, which has a soft handle and slight sheen. Bulk thread is similar but without the sheen. Use it on the upper looper, which forms the stitches on the upper edge of the seam. It is ideal for lingerie, swimwear or fabrics with Lycra®.

PRESSING TOOLS

Pressing is very important when sewing and can make all the difference to how professional the finished garment looks. Always press a seam before sewing over it again, which will help to flatten seam allowances, smooth seams and embed the stitches.

To achieve well-pressed seams, use a good steam iron together with a pressing cloth to protect the fabric and prevent shine. Also press from the wrong side whenever possible. As well as a good iron, the following pressing aids are extremely helpful. If you intend to do any speed tailoring (see pp. 122–133), it would be especially worth investing in a seam/sleeve roll and/or a sleeve board.

SEWING SENSE
Before using steam, test a sample of the fabric first and always use a pressing cloth when pressing delicate or textured fabric. Organza makes an excellent pressing cloth as it can withstand hot temperatures and is transparent so you can what you are pressing.

A **seam/sleeve roll** is a stuffed sausage shape that can be used to press sleeves without getting an imprint of the sleeve seam on the right side, as well as for pressing seams on yokes. These rolls are available ready-made, but you can also make one from medium-weight fabric. Join two 17 x 3in (43 x 7.5cm) pieces of fabric and stuff them firmly with wadding. A **sleeve board** makes a good substitute and looks like a mini-ironing board.

EXPERT TIP
If you don't have a seam roll or sleeve board,
a tightly rolled towel works just as well.

Tailor's ham This well-stuffed aid shaped like a ham is used to press open and shape seams, darts, etc., keeping the shape rather than flattening it. A ham can be purchased ready-made or made from medium-weight fabric. Join two 10 x 6in (25 x 15cm) oval pieces of fabric and stuff them firmly with wadding.

Needle board and pressing pad To avoid crushing pile on textured fabrics such as velvet or fleece, it is better to press with the fabric face down on a needle board, which is a pad covered with steel wires. An alternative is a velvet mat, which is a soft pad of pile fabric. Pressing a pile face down on the board will push it into the board rather than flatten it. A pressing pad made of wadded fabric can be used to press delicate fabrics embellished with beading or embroideries. A good substitute is a soft fluffy towel.

Pressing board, point pressers and **clappers** Pressing boards have various curved edges to help press collars, cuffs, etc. Some also incorporate point pressers. The clappers are heavy wooden blocks used to pound creases into heavyweight fabrics after they are steamed. Sometimes these are combined to make a pressing board/clapper.

PRESSING TECHNIQUES

- Press every seam before sewing over it again.
- Allow pressed items to cool properly before handling, particularly for preventing loose weaves and stretch fabrics stretching out of shape.
- Remember pressing is different from ironing. Place the iron on the fabric and gently move it very slightly. Then lift the iron and place it down again (rather than sliding it side to side). Repeat to press the whole piece.

SEWING SENSE
To save time, stitch all vertical seams and
then press in one batch.

SEWING MACHINES

We are in an enviable position nowadays as modern sewing machines make sewing a breeze. There's everything from simple machines that offer a few decorative stitches to all singing and dancing computerized sewing/embroidery machines that do everything. Deciding which is right for you will depend on your budget and the type of sewing you enjoy.

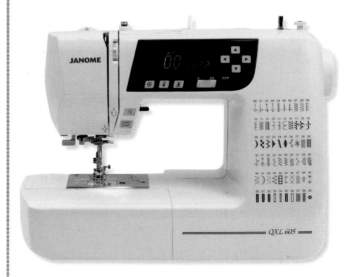

Modern machines are designed to make sewing simpler, with even the basic models having a selection of stitches and either a four- or one-step buttonhole ('four-step' involves turning a dial for each part of the buttonhole to be automatically stitched; 'one-step' means the machine will sew the complete buttonhole with one press of the button). Most modern machines are also self-lubricating, so you don't need to oil them regularly, although they do still need to be serviced professionally. The tension has such great tolerance that it's hard to get it wrong and you can sew from a single layer of flimsy fabric through to thick layers of heavyweight denim with ease. (The tension is correct when the bobbin thread is on the underside of the fabric and the top thread on the top, with the threads interlocking between the layers).

EXPERT TIP

If you do need to change the tension, do so a very little at a time. Then remember to return the tension dial to the standard setting (usually indicated on the dial) when returning to general sewing.

BUYING GUIDE

Decide on your budget and then within that choose a machine that can do all the things you might want to do in the future.

- If you want to quilt or make soft furnishings, choose a machine with a large sewing space between machine and needle.
- If dressmaking, select a model that has a good selection of stitches and a range of presser feet to cope with all sorts of fabrics.
- If you love embroidery, consider an embroidery machine or a sewing/embroidery machine.

TOP FEATURES TO LOOK FOR

- a range of straight and sideways (zigzag) stitches
- stitch width and length dials so you can change these to alter the stitches
- one-step (or four-step) buttonhole function
- a range of presser feet for different applications and fabrics
- stop/start button close to the needle
- a computerized model. This will be very simple to use and does so much automatically that it takes some of the guesswork out of choosing the correct presser foot or stitch length and width. Once a stitch is selected, the machine will automatically set the optimum length and width, and show on the screen which foot to use, although you can override these choices if you wish.

See the diagram on p. 19 for an outline of the features and functions on most modern machines.

PRESSER FEET

Most machines come with a selection of presser feet as completing specific tasks is much easier if you use the appropriate foot. For example, a zipper foot has indentations so you can get close to the zipper teeth and a blind hem foot has a little ledge to butt up against the hem. Here are the presser feet useful for dressmaking.

General-purpose foot Used for most sewing and dressmaking, this foot generally has two equal length toes and a gap in the centre through which the needle drops for straight and zigzag stitching.

GENERAL-PURPOSE FOOT   SATIN STICH FOOT

Satin stitch foot This is used for zigzag and sideways stitching, and particularly satin stitch, which is a very close, dense zigzag. The foot has a slight indentation on the underside so it slides smoothly over the dense stitching.

ZIPPER FOOT   BLIND HEM FOOT

Zipper foot Used for inserting zippers and attaching piping, this foot usually has a central toe with indentations on each side for the needle to slide through, so that you can stitch close to the bulky zipper or piping.

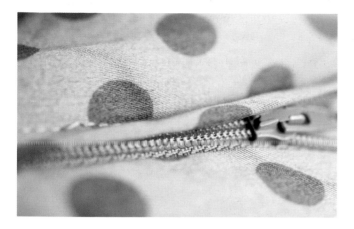

Blind hem foot Used to stitch blind/invisible hems, this foot generally has a wider left toe, with a little protruding downward ledge or brush, and a narrow right toe. The ledge is butted up against the folded fabric as you sew.

Buttonhole foot Many machines have a special buttonhole foot into which you place the button, so that the correct size hole is stitched automatically. The underside will have deep indentations to help feed the buttonhole stitching smoothly.

Overcasting foot Designed for neatening fabric edges, there will usually be a brush to the right of the foot that runs along the edge of the fabric, preventing it from rolling or puckering as you sew.

Walking foot Not always a standard feature, this cumbersome-looking foot is very useful for sewing plaids, checks and bulky pile fabrics. The feed dogs on the foot work in conjunction with the machine's feed dogs to feed both layers of fabric through evenly and smoothly so that one layer doesn't slip in relation to the other. It's worth investing in this foot if you sew fleece, wools or quilts.

BUTTONHOLE FOOT   OVERCASTING FOOT

WALKING FOOT

FEATURES AND FUNCTIONS ON SEWING MACHINES

Most features on a sewing machine are the same, no matter which model or brand. However, they might be in slightly different places, so check your user manual for specifics.

Thread spindle may be vertical or horizontal. The top thread reel is placed on the spindle and held in place with a thread retainer. Use this retainer to prevent the reel bouncing up and down as you sew, which can cause skipped stitches.

Upper thread guide is usually numbered to help feed the thread through the tension discs in the right order. Always have the presser foot raised when threading as this will release the internal tension discs so that the thread will easily fall between them as you thread up.

Thread tension dial shows the tension for the upper thread. A regular tension (for most fabrics) is usually indicated on the dial.

Needle holder has a screw to the inner side, which needs to be tightened with a screwdriver (supplied as part of the machine's tool kit) once the needle is in place. Needles are generally inserted with the flat part of the shank to the back of the needle holder.

Presser foot is lowered by the lever to the right of the needle holder, also engaging the tension discs. Once lowered, the foot will gently hold fabric in place. It holds the fabric down, working in conjunction with the feed dogs to guide the fabric through. Presser feet often clip or snap on and so are easy to remove and replace.

Throat plate (also known as needle plate) may be metal or clear plastic. It has a hole through which the needle drops to pick up the bobbin thread and also has holes for the feed dogs to raise and lower as you sew. It usually has markings for various seam allowances to help guide the fabric evenly.

SEWING SENSE
To prevent lightweight fabrics being pulled down into the throat plate at the start of a seam, hold the bobbin and top threads behind the needle as you begin to stitch.

Feed dogs are the jagged tracks that protrude through the throat plate. These move back and forth, up and down as you sew to help move the fabric along. On most machines, they can be lowered, and thus become inoperative, for free-motion sewing so you can move the fabric to determine the direction of stitching.

Bobbin case and **bobbin** can drop in (seated below the throat plate) or be front-loading in a special shuttle. Bobbins are either metal or clear plastic. Drop-in bobbins are simple to use and with many you can see easily how much thread is left. Keep the bobbin area clean and fluff free using the little brush provided. Always use bobbins designed for your brand of machine because, although they look identical, they can be slightly different and the wrong ones may not perform properly. The bobbin thread interlocks with the top thread to form stitches.

Flatbed is the wider bed around the needle plate, which helps keep the fabric flat as you sew. Usually the wider bed can be removed to reveal a narrower arm, so that small circular items like cuffs can be sewn easily.

Bobbin winding spindle is a two-part mechanism, consisting of a short metal spindle with a lever that is pushed towards the spindle once a bobbin is in place. On most machines this will automatically disengage the needle (advisable to avoid breaking it), so as you press the presser foot, the bobbin winds with thread but the needle remains stationery. If not, you might have to pull out part of the flywheel to disengage the needle.

Flywheel/balance wheel, on the right side of the machine, is turned towards you to raise and lower the needle by hand to take one stitch at a time. Some basic models may have an inner/outer ring that is pulled out to disengage the needle for bobbin winding.

Stitch selection offers the choice of built-in stitches available on the machine. These are accessed by turning a dial or selecting a combination of buttons.

Stitch length is shown by a dashed line. Increasing the stitch length makes longer stitches, suitable for thick layers; decreasing it makes shorter stitches, appropriate for very fine fabrics.

Stitch width is shown with a zizag line. This will alter the width of sideways stitches. Increasing the width makes the stitches wider; decreasing it makes them narrower.

EXPERT TIP

Different stitches may require the needle to be in a slightly different position. So when you change the stitch selection, raise the needle to prevent it bending or breaking in the throat plate. Also try out the new stitch, turning the balance wheel by hand to ensure the needle will go cleanly through the presser foot and throat plate.

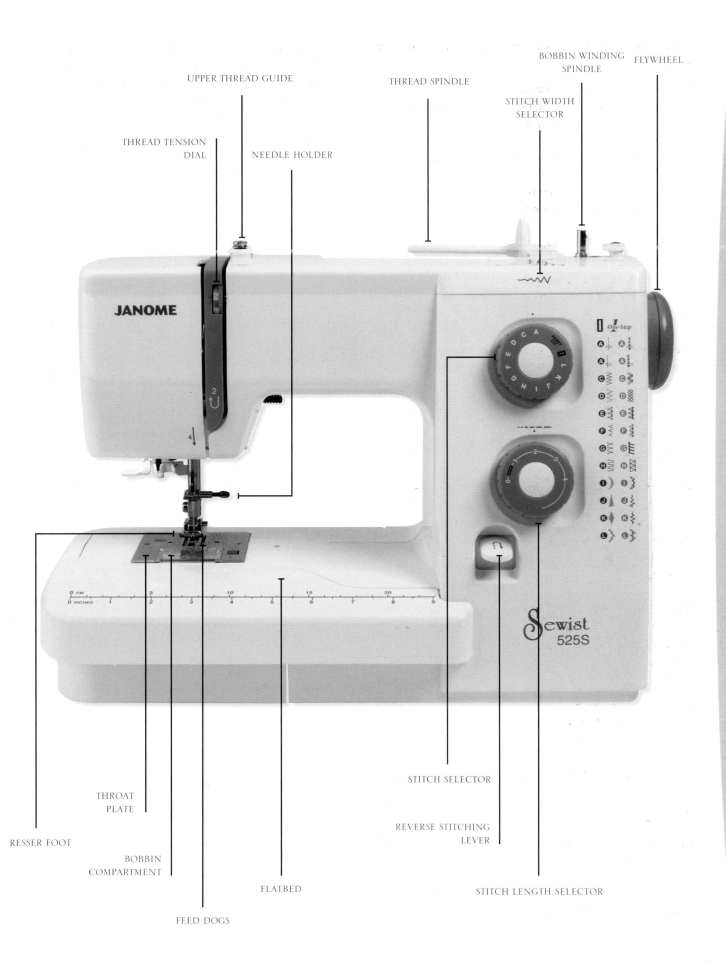

UPPER THREAD GUIDE

THREAD SPINDLE

BOBBIN WINDING SPINDLE

FLYWHEEL

STITCH WIDTH SELECTOR

THREAD TENSION DIAL

NEEDLE HOLDER

JANOME

Sewist 525S

STITCH SELECTOR

REVERSE STITCHING LEVER

STITCH LENGTH SELECTOR

THROAT PLATE

RESSER FOOT

BOBBIN COMPARTMENT

FLATBED

FEED DOGS

Sergers (overlockers)

These are much undervalued machines, which sew and neaten seams in one pass and are particularly useful for sewing knit fabrics. However, they are really an additional machine to have – not a replacement for a sewing machine – as they cannot do buttonholes, darts, etc.

A serger can use between three and eight threads, depending on the model and brand (three-thread types are the simplest to use). Each thread has its own path and tension. Straight stitches, formed by the needles, combine with overcast edges, made by the upper and lower loopers. The stitches are flexible and so ideal for stretch fabrics. A serger also has a knife, which cuts excess fabric from the seam allowance just before it is stitched and overlocked, making it a one-step sewing and neatening operation. (The knife can be disengaged for decorative stitching, flat locking, etc.)

SEWING SENSE

Some machines like to be threaded in a certain order and will continually unthread themselves or break threads if this isn't followed! Check your user manual.

FEATURES AND FUNCTIONS OF SERGERS

Loopers upper and lower, wrap threads around the cut fabric edge as it is stitched. The threads are guided through the relevant tension discs and come up from inside the machine. The loopers use the most thread (see Threads, p. 13 for more information).

Needles (two) are used to stitch two parallel straight rows, the right one interlinking with the looper threads. You can use the same needles as for sewing machines. Sometimes the left needle is removed so that different stitch patterns can be formed, for example, for rolled hems and flat locking.

Knife blade is sited just in front of the needles so that as the fabric is fed through, the blade cuts the excess seam allowance just before the fabric is stitched. The knife can be disengaged for specialist stitching.

Presser foot can be left down even at the start of stitching as the powerful feed dogs will feed the fabric easily. Different presser feet are available for different techniques, but most machines come with one standard foot.

Thread holders extend up or can be pushed down for storage and help to feed the threads smoothly. At the base are long spindles to hold the big cones of thread.

Balance wheel can be turned to raise and lower the needles and form stitches one by one.

Looper thread guides are positioned under a panel on the front of the machine. They are usually colour-coded so you can see which thread goes through which guide. The lower looper is the most fiddly.

EXPERT TIP
To rethread quickly, cut the thread near the cone and tie new thread to the one already threaded up. Sew the thread tail until the new thread appears. For needle thread, sew until the knot gets close to the needle eye, then stop, cut the knot away and thread manually.

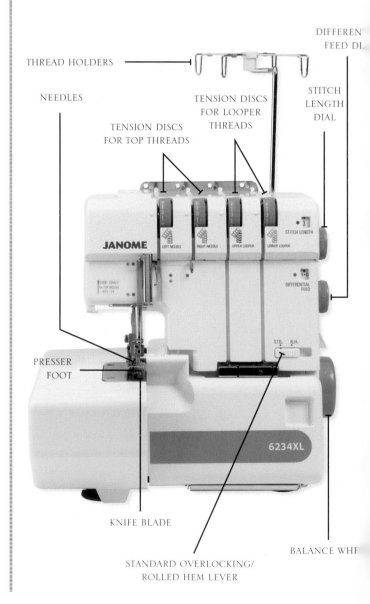

THREAD HOLDERS

NEEDLES

TENSION DISCS FOR LOOPER THREADS

TENSION DISCS FOR TOP THREADS

DIFFEREN FEED DI

STITCH LENGTH DIAL

PRESSER FOOT

KNIFE BLADE

STANDARD OVERLOCKING/ ROLLED HEM LEVER

BALANCE WHE

Wish list of tools and equipment

MISCELLANEOUS

Metre rule A straight, wooden rule is useful when measuring long lengths, marking grain lines, extending pattern pieces, etc.

Double-sided basting tape with adhesive on both sides provides a quick and easy alternative to using basting stitches. Generally, one side is paper-backed to protect the adhesive.

Fray stop or **fabric adhesive** is extremely useful for preventing fabric from fraying especially when you need to clip in toward a seam at a corner.

French curve This can either be a transparent plastic measuring tool with curved sides or simply a flexible plastic-covered rod that can be manipulated into the shape you require. This is handy if you are redrawing armholes, pockets, etc.

Point turner Made from wood or plastic, this is a particularly useful gadget for helping to push out corners on collars, pockets, cuffs, etc. Some are marked with imperial and metric measurements and so can also be used to turn up hem allowances. You could use a knitting needle, carefully, as a substitute.

Rouleau turner This specialist tool is a long, thin rod with a tiny hook at one end and makes turning through spaghetti straps a breeze. The hook end of the rod is pushed into the fabric tube, sewn right sides together. The hook is then clipped onto the end of the fabric tube and the rod is pulled back through the tube, bringing the clipped end with it, turning the fabric through.

SCISSORS

Spring-touch scissors The handles on these are positioned one above the other and spring open between cuts. They can be used right or left-handed and are comfortable to use over prolonged periods.

Duck-billed scissors Also known as appliqué scissors, one blade has a curved flat end which slides along the base fabric as you safely cut the appliqué fabric edge on the top. They are also useful to grade seam allowances (see p. 26).

Scissor sharpener This handy tool is used to remove nicks and burrs on scissor blades as well as sharpening them. (It cannot be used with pinking or dressmaking shears with serrated blades.)

NEEDLES

Quilting needles have a longer, sharper point to more easily penetrate several layers of fabric.

Leather needles have a triangular chiselled point to pierce leather, faux suede and other non-woven fabrics. The needle will leave holes, however, so only sew seams when sure of the fit. A wing needle is another type, which has a wider winged shaft in order to leave holes on each side of a stylized heirloom stitch.

Machine embroidery needles have a larger eye to cater for embroidery and novelty threads. They are also used for top stitching with top-stitching or decorative threads.

FOR PRESSING

Clapper In addition to the pressing aids on pp. 14–15, a clapper board is useful for tailoring and pressing sharp creases. It is a wooden block with different angles and curves over which creases can be formed and pressed.

BASIC SEWING SKILLS

GET STARTED WITH CONFIDENCE,
ARMED WITH SOME TIPS ON
SUCCESSFULLY SEWING AND SOME OF
THE BASIC STITCHES, SEAMS, SEAM
FINISHES AND HEMMING TECHNIQUES
THAT ARE FREQUENTLY USED
IN DRESSMAKING.

SEWING SENSE

*The diagrams in this book use
the following abbreviations for
quick reference:*

RS – right side of the fabric
SA – seam allowance
*WS – wrong side of
the fabric*

BASIC MACHINE STITCHES

With the following basic stitches at your fingertips, you will be ready and able to sew any garment. Many – and certainly the most important – of these stitches are available on even the most basic sewing machines.

STRAIGHT STITCH

The most useful and most commonly used stitch is quite simply a straight stitch. It's used to join two or more layers of fabric together and, if sewn as a seam in dressmaking, is normally stitched ⅝in (1.5cm) from the raw edges. As a general rule, a stitch length of 2.2–2.5 is perfect for most light- and medium-weight fabrics (equal to about 10 stitches per inch (2.5cm)). Heavier fabrics are best stitched with a longer stitch length of 3–3.5. A perfect stitch is formed when the top thread shows on the top of the seam and the bobbin thread on the underside. If the fabric puckers, the stitch length needs to be lengthened; if the fabric gathers easily, decrease the stitch length.

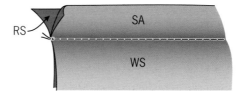

FIGURE 1 RUN THE MACHINE AT MEDIUM SPEED TO SEW ACCURATELY STRAIGHT ALONG THE SEAM LINE.

BACK STITCH

A straight stitch in reverse, back stitch is used to anchor stitching at the start and end of a seam. Your sewing machine will have a button or lever to hold down for reverse stitching.

1 Start about ¾in (2cm) in from the seam end and, holding the thread tails behind the needle, press the reverse button to stitch three or four stitches backwards.

2 Release the button and stitch forwards, continuing to the end of the seam.

3 Repeat the back stitching to finish the seam.

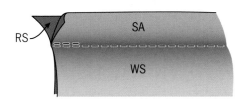

FIGURE 2 USE BACK STITCH TO SECURE THE STITCHING AT EACH END.

ZIGZAG STITCH

This is a sideways stitch used to neaten raw edges or to stitch stretch fabrics so that the stitching has some flexibility. Select the zigzag stitch option and then try it out. If necessary, decrease the stitch width to make the stitches narrower from side to side and/ or decrease the stitch length to bring the stitches closer together (very close zigzag stitches are called satin stitch). For a larger zigzag, simply increase the stitch length and/or width.

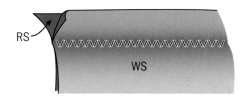

FIGURE 3 USE ZIGZAG STITCH TO NEATEN THE RAW EDGES AND STOP THEM FROM FRAYING.

OVERCAST STITCH

Overcasting is used to prevent fabric edges from fraying or unravelling. Many sewing machines have an overcast stitch among their utility/basic stitches. It is sewn on the seam allowance with the right swing of the stitch just over the edge of the fabric. If no overcast stitch is available, use zigzag stitch instead. For lightweight fabrics, reduce the stitch width; for heavier fabrics, choose a longer stitch length and width.

FIGURE 4 OVERCAST STITCH CAN ALSO BE USED TO NEATEN RAW EDGES AND STOP THEM FROM FRAYING.

EXPERT TIP

Overcast or zigzag stitch the seam allowances of all garment pieces before joining them together and sewing the seams. A serger (overlocker) is ideal for overlocking seam allowances quickly (see p. 34).

Tension

On most modern sewing machines the needle tension shouldn't need adjusting for dressmaking. If, however, you do find that the needle thread is showing too much on the wrong side of the fabric, then very slightly increase the tension according to instructions in the user manual. Test stitch on a remnant of the same fabric and number of layers as being used for the garment.

MACHINE BASTING

Use the longest stitch length and a contrast colour thread to machine baste seams together temporarily. As the stitching will be removed, the seam doesn't need securing at each end. A contrast colour thread makes it easier to see the stitching that needs to be removed.

STRETCH STITCH

This is a small slanted zigzag stitch used to sew stretch fabrics so that the seam retains some flexibility. If it's not available, a small zigzag stitch is equally effective.

FIGURE 5 THE STRETCH STITCH IS PERFECT FOR ALLOWING A SEAM TO STRETCH WITH A STRETCH FABRIC.

BASIC HAND STITCHES

Most of the basic stitches for dressmaking can be performed more quickly and easily on the machine. However, there are occasions when you might prefer to stitch by hand – slip stitching and blind hemming are particularly useful.

SLIP STITCH

Slip stitch can be used to hem lightweight fabrics, attach a lining to a zipper tape or close an opening. Small stitches are taken so that they are virtually invisible on the right side.

1 Secure the end of the thread within the fold of the hem or seam allowance.

2 Slip the needle through just one or two fibres of the main fabric and then up through the fabric fold at a slight angle to the left. Pull the thread through.

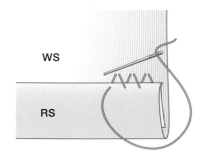

FIGURE 6 TAKE TINY STITCHES INTO THE MAIN FABRIC SO THEY ARE VIRTUALLY INVISIBLE.

3 Repeat this process to the end of the hem, keeping the stitches and tension even.

BLIND HEMMING

The effects of blind hemming are very similar to slip stitching, but the technique is more suitable for hemming heavier weight fabrics. It prevents an unsightly ridge along the top edge of the hem showing on the right side.

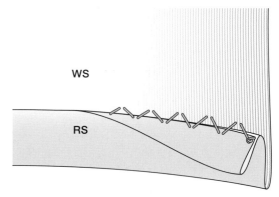

FIGURE 7 TAKE TINY STITCHES INTO THE MAIN FABRIC AND THE TURNED UNDER HEM ALLOWANCE.

MACHINE STITCHES FOR SPECIFIC TECHNIQUES

The following stitches are all formed using straight stitch, but have different names to identify their use in garment construction.

EASE STITCH

Ease stitch is used to fit a garment piece with slightly more fabric in the seam to a piece with less fabric in the seam, such as inserting a sleeve into an armhole or attaching the side front to the front of a blouse.

1 Set the stitch length slightly longer than the regular length, 3–5 depending on the fabric weight, so that the fabric can be gathered very slightly.

2 Stitch close to the seam line on the piece with more fabric, within the seam allowance.

3 Then pull up the bobbin thread to slightly gather the excess fabric to fit the other garment piece. Any gathers will be in the seam allowance and should not show on the right side once the seam is stitched and pressed.

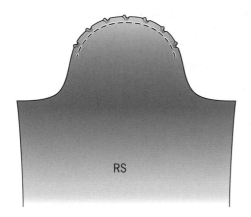

FIGURE 8 USE EASE STITCH TO TAKE UP THE FULLNESS OF FABRIC WITHOUT SHOWING ANY PUCKERS.

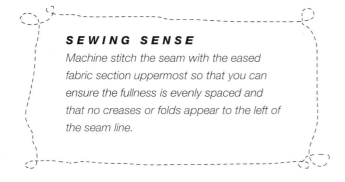

SEWING SENSE

Machine stitch the seam with the eased fabric section uppermost so that you can ensure the fullness is evenly spaced and that no creases or folds appear to the left of the seam line.

STAY STITCH

Also a straight stitch just inside the seam allowance, stay stitching is used to prevent the fabric stretching while constructing a garment. Use a regular stitch length: 2.2–2.5 for lightweight fabrics, 2.5–3 for medium and 3.5 for heavyweight. It is stitched on curved or bias cut areas, such as collars, V-necklines and front wraps, prior to seaming. As an alternative, you could fuse fusible stay stitching/edge tape to the seam allowance.

UNDER STITCH

This describes the stitching used to help keep seam allowances in place on collars, facings, etc.

1 After stitching a facing to the garment edge, grade the seam allowances (see p. 26) to reduce bulk and then press them towards the facing.

2 With the facing uppermost and keeping the garment out of the way, straight stitch the seam allowances to the facing.

3 Then fold and press the facing inside the garment, rolling the seam to the underside a little.

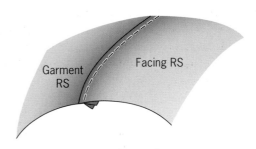

FIGURE 9 UNDER STITCH THE SEAM ALLOWANCES TO THE FACING TO KEEP THEM IN PLACE.

TOP STITCH

Quite simply, this is the term used for stitching that shows on the surface of the fabric. It is often used as a decorative feature, but also has the benefit of holding facings, hems, etc. in place on the underside. Top stitch thread can be in a colour to match the fabric so it is almost invisible or in a contrast colour to stand out as a feature.

1 Top stitch with a slightly longer stitch of 3.5 and either use the presser foot edge as a guide or draw a chalk line to follow.

2 Stitch approximately ⅜in (1cm) from the edge or seam.

EDGE STITCHING

This is the same as top stitching, but is stitched a scant ⅛in (3mm) from the edge and usually in a thread colour to match the fabric.

STITCH IN THE DITCH

This straight stitch is another way to keep the under layer in place and is formed along the line of the previous seaming. It is used to hold a folded-over waistband or bias binding in place. Stitch slowly, with a thread in colour to match the fabric, slightly parting the previous seam as you go, letting the needle drop in the 'ditch'.

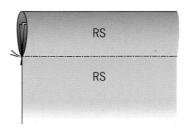

FIGURE 10 SECURE LAYERS TOGETHER BY STITCHING IN THE 'DITCH' MADE BY THE PREVIOUS SEAM.

COMMON SEWING TECHNIQUES

The following frequently used techniques will help you achieve a professional fit and finish.

CLIPPING AND NOTCHING

It is often advisable to clip or notch seam allowances once the seams are sewn, particularly around curved seams, in order for them to lie smoothly and flat. If left unclipped, the seam allowance would otherwise bunch up or be stretched, causing unsightly gathers or lumps.

Seams that have an inner curve are clipped with an angled snip into the seam allowance every 1–1½in (2.5–3 cm). Clip up to but not through the seam stitching. Once turned through, the cut edges will spread and thus not stretch the seam unduly.

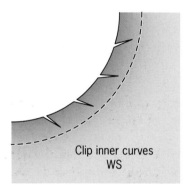

Clip inner curves
WS

FIGURE 11 CLIP ACROSS THE SEAM ALLOWANCE TO GIVE THE SEAM ON AN INNER CURVE MORE FLEXIBILITY.

Wedge-shaped notches are snipped out of outer curved seams so that when turned through, the cut edges close up and the seam allowance doesn't cause bumps. Again, cut up to but not through the seam stitching, making notches every 2–3in (5–8cm), or more frequently on bulky fabrics

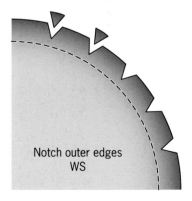

Notch outer edges
WS

FIGURE 12 NOTCH INTO THE SEAM ALLOWANCE TO REDUCE EXCESS FABRIC ON AN OUTER CURVE.

GRADING SEAMS

Seam allowances are trimmed to different widths in order to reduce bulk within the fold of the seam, particularly when attaching facings, collars, cuffs, waistbands, etc. The seam allowance furthest from the garment fabric is cut to a scant ⅛–⅜in (3mm–1cm), while the one that lies closes to the main fabric is cut to approximately ¼–⅝in (6mm–1.5cm).

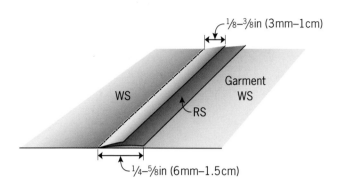

⅛–⅜in (3mm–1cm)

WS

Garment
WS

RS

¼–⅝in (6mm–1.5cm)

FIGURE 13 TRIM AWAY VARYING AMOUNTS OF SEAM ALLOWANCES TO REDUCE BULK.

PIN BASTING

A quick alternative to machine basting (see p. 24), particularly on straight seams, pins can also be used to temporarily baste seams together. Use pins with glass or plastic heads, which you can remove easily as you sew, and pin at right angles to the seam. If sewing with slippery fabrics, pin more frequently and remove the pins as you get to them.

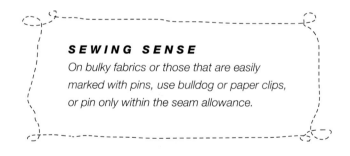

SEWING SENSE

On bulky fabrics or those that are easily marked with pins, use bulldog or paper clips, or pin only within the seam allowance.

BASIC SEAMS

There are some basic seams (and seam finishes; see p. 28) that are frequently used in dressmaking and are easily mastered. The seams include straight stitched seams and lapped, welt and French seams. The best one to use depends on the fabric and garment.

Seams are sewn with a seam allowance, usually ⅝in (1.5cm) in dressmaking. The seam allowance ensures the stitching is not on the very edge of the fabric, allows room for handling, prevents seams pulling apart and thus enables the seam to maintain shape. The allowance can also be used to accommodate slight adjustments in fit.

Seams are generally sewn with the right sides of the fabric together and edges matching. Hold the thread tails behind the needle at the start of the seam to prevent them tangling or lightweight fabrics been pulled into the hole in the throat plate of the sewing machine. Wherever possible, stitch all seams in the same direction to prevent them twisting or pulling out of shape. Also press every seam before stitching over it again, pressing from the wrong side and then from the right side.

STRAIGHT STITCH SEAM

This most commonly used seam is sewn with a straight stitch ⅝in (1.5cm) from the fabric edge, with the right sides of the fabric together. The stitch length depends on the fabric thickness (see Straight stitch, p. 22). Neaten the seam allowances once the seam is pressed.

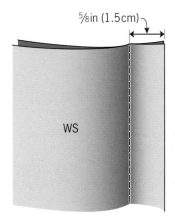

⅝in (1.5cm)

WS

FIGURE 14 ALLOW ⅝ IN (1.5CM) SEAM ALLOWANCES IN MOST SEAMS.

STRETCH SEAM

Stretch stitch is used for joining stretch knit fabrics together when the seam needs to stretch without the thread breaking (for example, for pulling the garment over the head, etc.). Most machines have a stretch stitch (see p. 24), which is an angled zigzag, but if not, a small zigzag stitch works just as well. Stretch fabrics don't necessarily need neatening because they will not unravel. However, they do sometimes curl so can be stitched with a double stitched seam (see right) or finished with a wider zigzag and then trimmed close to the stitching.

EXPERT TIP
When working with knits, stabilize the areas that should not stretch, such as the neckline and shoulders, with stay stitching (see p. 25) or fusible edge tape within the seam allowance.

DOUBLE STITCHED SEAM

Two rows of stitching are sewn for a double stitched seam, one on the seam line and the other a scant ⅛in (3mm) away, within the seam allowance. The second row of stitching can be straight or zigzag if the fabric frays badly. This provides a very durable seam, makes a narrow seam on lightweight transparent fabrics or lace, or is used on knit fabrics to prevent the edges curling.

BIAS SEAM

When stitching bias-cut fabric, the seaming can stretch and buckle. To prevent this, slightly stretch the fabric behind and in front of the needle as you sew. Once pressed, the stitching will relax into a smooth seam. If sewing a heavyweight fabric cut on the bias, consider stitching a twill tape to the seam line to prevent it sagging and drooping.

FRENCH SEAM

A French seam produces a very neat finish and is ideal on transparent fabrics where the underside is clearly visible.

1 Sew the seam with the wrong sides of the fabric together, taking a narrow ⅜in (1cm) seam allowance.

2 Trim the seam allowances to ⅛in (3mm) and turn through so the right sides are together and the seam line is on the fold.

3 Press, then stitch again, taking a ¼in (6mm) seam allowance, thus neatly encasing the raw edges of the trimmed seam.

RS

¼in (6mm)
⅛in (3mm)

WS

FIGURE 15 ENCASE THE RAW EDGES WITHIN THE FRENCH SEAM.

LAPPED SEAM

As the name suggests, here the seam allowances are lapped so one is on top of the other. It is a useful seam for fabrics, such as faux suede and leather, which don't fray.

1 Mark the seam allowance on the layer that will overlap with a chalk line. For vertical seams, lap away from the centre; for horizontal seams, lap downwards.

2 Trim away the marked seam allowance and lay the fabric over the unmarked piece, so that the cut edge just overlaps the underlayer's seam allowance.

3 Edge stitch close to the trimmed edge and then stitch again, ⅜in (1cm) away, catching the underlap in place both times.

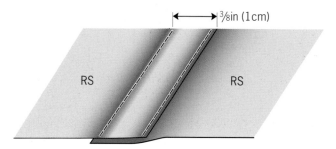

FIGURE 16 EDGE STITCH AND TOP STITCH THE LAPPED SEAM.

FLAT FELL SEAM

This type of seam, stitched and neatened on both sides, is often used on sportswear and reversible garments.

1 Stitch the seam with the fabric wrong sides together, taking a regular seam allowance.

2 Press both seam allowances to one side before trimming the under allowance to a scant ⅛in (3mm).

3 On the upper seam allowance, turn under the edge by ¼in (6mm) and then pin and edge stitch it in place, encasing the lower allowance as you go.

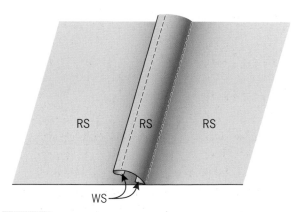

FIGURE 17 FOLD THE WIDER SEAM ALLOWANCE OVER TO CONCEAL THE RAW EDGES ON A FLAT FELL SEAM.

SEAM FINISHES

Once a seam is stitched, the seam allowance needs to be neatened either to prevent fraying or to provide a clean finish, if it isn't encased in the seam, on the inside of a garment. Different finishes suit different fabrics and garments, and range from simple pinked seams to encased seam allowances or double welt seams.

PINKED SEAM

Pinking is useful for fashion garments stitched in cotton and other light- to medium-weight fabrics that are not meant to last forever. The seam allowances are cut with pinking shears quite simply to prevent them from fraying.

OVERCAST/OVERLOCKED SEAM

The seam allowances are stitched with a special overcast stitch (see p. 23) or overlocked on a serger (see p. 34). On light- or medium-weight fabrics, they can be treated as one and neatened together. On heavier weight fabrics, it is better to press the seam allowances open and to neaten them individually.

BOUND SEAM ALLOWANCES

Also known as Hong Kong finish, the seam allowances are trimmed and then encased within a lightweight bias binding. It's a neat and attractive finish for unlined jackets or other garments where the inside might show. It's best to use a special lightweight stretchy seam binding tape that will automatically curl as it is stretched, wrapping itself around the seam allowance so you can stitch through both layers in one pass.

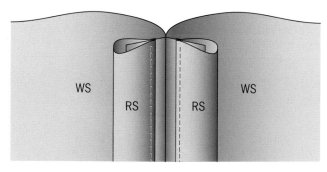

FIGURE 18 BIND THE SEAM ALLOWANCES WITH LIGHTWEIGHT BIAS BINDING.

WELT AND DOUBLE WELT SEAMS

Both these terms are used for the top stitching that is visible on the right side next to a seam, holding the seam allowances in place. Both are stitched with a regular seam. For a welt seam, press the seam allowances to one side and grade them (see p. 26). Then stitch ¼in (6mm) from the seam, catching the seam allowances underneath. For heavier weight fabrics, make a double welt seam by pressing the seam allowances open and stitching an equal distance on each side of the seam, again catching the seam allowances in place underneath.

Hemming techniques

Hemming is usually the technique used to complete a garment so it is worth considering what method works best depending on the fabric and type of garment. The hemming tips below will also ensure that the finished garment hangs beautifully.

HEMMING TIPS

Let the garment hang for 24 hours before hemming, particularly if working with stretch knit fabric or a garment cut on the bias. This allows the fabric to drop and settle so that the edge can be cut level before hemming.

To determine the hem length, measure up from the floor to the desired length, wearing the heel height that will be worn with the outfit, to ensure that the hem is level all round.

Mark the hem length with horizontally placed pins, holding up the allowance with pins placed vertically. Cut the hem allowance evenly all the way round.

If hemming jackets or tailored skirts and dresses, consider adding hem weights to the hem allowance, which will help the hem hang straight. Hem weights can be fine chain laid in the hem fold or small button-shaped discs sewn at the front edges and back seams.

The amount of hem allowance depends on the garment and fabric, but as a general rule, allow a narrower hem of 1¼–2 in (3– 5cm) for trousers and A-line skirts or dresses, while for straight dresses, skirts, jackets and coats allow 2–3in (5–7.5cm).

Once the correct length has been determined and the hem allowance marked, it is time to finish the hem, using one of these methods on the right or on pp. 30–31.

SEWING SENSE

Once the hem is pinned in place, try the garment on again before committing to stitch.

HANDLING CURVED HEMS

Garments that are full skirted, A-line or cut on the bias will have a curved hem, which has extra fullness that needs to be eased into the hem allowance to avoid bumps and ridges on the right side.

1 Ease stitch (see p. 24) about ¼in (6mm) from the raw hem edge.

2 Gently gather the hem allowance by pulling up the bobbin thread.

3 Spread the gathers evenly and turn up the hem, so that the gathers are only in the hem allowance.

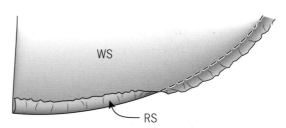

FIGURE 19 USE EASE STITCH TO GENTLY GATHER THE RAW EDGE AND PRODUCE A PERFECTLY SMOOTH CURVED HEM.

TOP-STITCHED HEM

This is the easiest and quickest hem finish. Linings are usually stitched with a top-stitched hem and should finish just above the main garment hem.

1 Fold the hem allowance up at the hem depth and then fold it in again so the raw edge meets the first fold and is encased. If working with heavyweight fabrics, neaten the raw edge of the hem allowance before turning it up so it doesn't need to be folded under again.

2 Pin the hem in place and stitch from the right side close to the inner fold. You can use matching thread so the stitching is almost invisible or contrast thread and a decorative stitch to make a feature of the stitching.

FIGURE 20 TOP-STITCH HEMS WITH MATCHING OR CONTRASTING THREAD

EXPERT TIP

Use a twin needle to create a top-stitched hem that looks like the cover-stitch found on ready-to-wear garments. Alter the tension to 7 and use two spools of thread for the needles. The bobbin thread will then zigzag between the two to create a zigzag stitch underneath, with two perfectly parallel rows on the top.

BLIND HEM

This is a good choice of hem for medium- to heavyweight fabrics, smart clothes, jackets, dresses, trousers, etc. The hem is turned up and sewn so that all that is visible from the right side is a tiny ladder stitch.

1 Neaten the raw edge and then turn up the hem allowance.

2 Fold the hem allowance back on itself so that about ¼–½in (6mm–1.3cm) protrudes to the right.

3 Attach a blind hem foot, which has a guide to sit the folded fabric against, to the machine and select blind hem stitch (a row of straight stitches regularly interspersed with zigzag stitches). Stitch the hem: the straight stitches of the blind hem stitch are formed in the hem allowance and then every so often the zigzag swings to the left to catch the garment.

4 Flatten out the hem and press with a press cloth to embed the stitches.

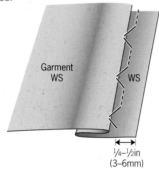

Garment WS

WS

¼–½in (3–6mm)

FIGURE 21 USE THE BLIND HEM FUNCTION ON YOUR MACHINE FOR AN INVISIBLE FINISH.

EXPERT TIP

Avoid pressing the actual hem edge as blind hems should have a soft, rounded edge.

BOUND HEM

This is another technique that works well with tailored garments or heavyweight fabrics where a single turn of hem allowance is preferred.

1 Open out the hem allowance and stitch bias binding to the right side of the raw hem edge.

2 Press and then fold up the hem allowance.

3 Either blind stitch or hand stitch the binding to the inside of the garment.

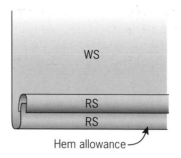

WS

RS

RS

Hem allowance

FIGURE 22 USE BIAS BINDING TO BIND A HEM WITHOUT ADDING MUCH BULK.

TAILORED HEM

Adding a strip of interfacing to the wrong side of the garment within the hem allowance will help the drape of tailored garments, producing a lovely crisp finish.

1 Cut a length of fusible interfacing the width of the hem allowance and press it in place.

2 Neaten the raw edge of the hem with overcast stitch or with bias binding.

3 Turn up and then blind hem or hand stitch the hem allowance to the interfacing only. This ensures that there are no stitches visible on the right side. Adding dress weights will also aid the drape.

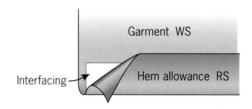

Garment WS

Hem allowance RS

Interfacing

FIGURE 23 SEW THE HEM ALLOWANCE TO A STRIP OF INTERFACING TO PRODUCE AN INVISIBLE HEM ON TAILORED GARMENTS.

ROLLED HEM

This type of hem is particularly suited to lightweight and transparent fabrics where the hem allowance would be visible. The hem allowance is minimal, a scant ¼in (6mm). Using a rolled hem foot is ideal as the front of the presser foot has a curl through which the fabric edge is fed and rolled as it is stitched close to the edge. However, a rolled hem can be stitched without a specialist foot.

FIGURE 24 MAKE SURE YOUR ROLLED HEM IS VERY NARROW.

1 Press up a ⅛in (3mm) hem allowance and stitch close to the fold. Trim any excess hem allowance away.

2 Fold up again so the stitching is just inside the hem allowance. Press and pin.

3 Stitch the hem again close to the inner fold.

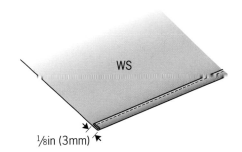

⅛in (3mm)

LETTUCE EDGING

This treatment works best on stretch knit fabrics or those cut on the bias with lots of stretch. As you stitch with a very close, small zigzag stitch, pull the fabric taut behind and in front of the needle, stretching it as you sew. Once released the fabric will gather into attractive flutes.

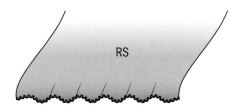

RS

FIGURE 25 USE A TINY ZIGZAG STITCH TO HEM STRETCHY FABRICS AND PRODUCE AN ATTRACTIVE FLUTED LETTUCE HEM EDGE.

EXPERT TIP

Avoid stitching hems into leather and suede by using fusible hemming web instead. Allow just ⅝in (1.5cm) of hem allowance and turn up. Place the hemming web in between the layers and, using a press cloth, press with a medium hot, dry iron. For heavyweight leather or suede, leave the hem edge unfinished by simply cutting the hem allowance off.

HANDLING CURVES AND CORNERS

When sewing collars, cuffs, shaped necklines, pockets, etc., you will come across curves and corners. To ensure a perfectly stitched finish, follow these steps.

HANDLING CURVES

Fabrics cut on the curve or at an angle will have part of the edge cut on the bias, which is the stretchiest part of the fabric. To prevent unwanted stretch in seams, it is therefore necessary to stablize the fabric before joining the pieces. This is particularly important at shoulders and neck edges, for example, on the front edges of wrap tops. To do this, stay stitch (see p. 25) just within the seam allowance or fuse an edge tape to the seam allowance.

If the curved seam has a facing and will be turned through once stitched, it is also necessary to clip and notch the seam allowance so that the seam lies flat. For outer curves, take notches and for inner curves, clip into the seam allowance regularly (see p. 26).

HANDLING CORNERS

There is a lot of seam allowance coming together in a small area at a corner so the bulk has to be reduced. Corners also often come under extra stress so the stitching needs strengthening.

1 To make a strong, perfectly shaped corner, first stitch with a regular stitch to within 1in (2.5cm) of the corner, then reduce the stitch length by 0.5–1 and sew to the corner.

2 With the needle down, raise the presser foot and pivot the work to take one stitch at an angle across the point of the corner. Again with the needle down, raise the presser foot to pivot the work in line with the next seam line.

3 Then stitch for 1in (2.5cm) before increasing the stitch length again and continuing with the seam.

4 To reduce the bulk, trim the seam allowances straight across the corner. Then trim the seam allowances on each side, curving into the corner for the last inch (2.5cm). For bulky fabrics, also grade the seam allowances (see p. 26). Dab a little fabric adhesive or fray stop to the very tip of the corner. Once dried, turn the corner out, pushing out the point using a point turner.

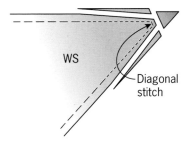

WS

Diagonal stitch

FIGURE 26 PLACE A TINY STITCH DIAGONALLY ACROSS A CORNER AND, WHEN THE SEAM IS COMPLETED, TRIM THE EXCESS FABRIC.

MITRING

This technique provides a very neatly turned corner on patch pockets, at hem edges, or on surface-mounted trims.

1 Fold the seam allowances on both edges of the corner to the wrong side and press. Unfold the seam allowances. Then turn in and press the corner diagonally where the two previous creases cross.

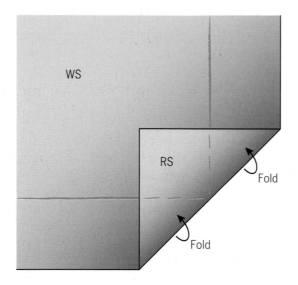

FIGURE 27 FOLD THE CORNER SO THE FOLD IS AT A 45-DEGREE ANGLE TO THE SEAM LINES.

2 Unfold the corner. With right sides together, refold the fabric, bringing the side edges together. Stitch across the corner diagonally, following the creased line. Trim the corner close to the seam.

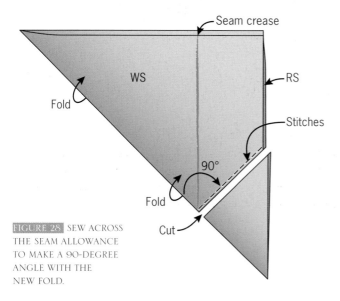

FIGURE 28 SEW ACROSS THE SEAM ALLOWANCE TO MAKE A 90-DEGREE ANGLE WITH THE NEW FOLD.

3 Press again, opening out the narrow seam allowances. Turn through, pushing the corner out with a point turner.

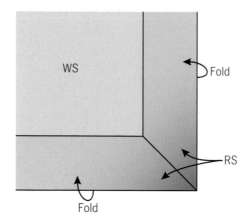

FIGURE 29 FOLD THE SEAM ALLOWANCES UNDER, PUSHING THE MITRED CORNER OUT.

GATHERS AND RUFFLES

Gathers are used to add fullness to a garment by pulling up a longer piece of fabric to fit a shorter piece. Ruffles are gathered sections added as a decorative finish on sleeves, hems or neck edges. Both can be stitched easily with a little know how.

MAKING GATHERS

1 Prepare the fabric by stitching a row of the longest stitch length possible just within the seam allowance. Start at one end, leaving long thread tails and stitch to the other, again leaving thread tails. If gathering a long piece of fabric of over ½yd (50cm), stitch it in two or three sections, each time leaving long thread tails at the start and end of the row of stitching. On heavier weight fabrics, sew two parallel rows of stitching.

2 Pull up the bobbin thread to gather the fabric, gently easing the gathers along the stitching until the correct length is achieved. Then wind the spare thread around a pin to anchor it or thread it onto a needle and stitch it on the spot to secure.

3 Pin the gathered fabric to the straight edge piece, right sides together and sew the seam, with the gathered piece uppermost so you can guide it under the presser foot evenly.

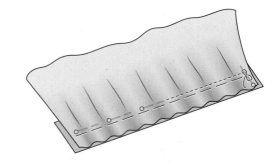

FIGURE 30 ADJUST THE GATHERS EVENLY AND STITCH THE GATHERED FABRIC TO THE MAIN GARMENT PIECE.

4 Turn the gathered piece down to the right side. Press the seam allowances away from the gathered piece and, if desired, top stitch (see p. 25) close to the seam line to keep the seam allowances in place.

(see p. 25)

SEWING SENSE

When gathering, use a contrast colour thread in the bobbin so it is easy to identify it.

EXPERT TIP

If gathering heavyweight fabric or long strips, use the cord method. Lay a length of string or cord just inside the seam line and zigzag stitch over it, without catching it in the stitching. To gather the fabric, anchor the cord at one end and then pull up the other end, adjusting the gathers as you go. Pin and stitch the gathered piece to the garment and then remove the cord.

MAKING RUFFLES

Ruffles are useful to add a decorative finish to a hem edge, on sleeves or to create a waterfall effect at a neckline. They are made from panels of fabric that are two to three times the length of the straight edge to which they will be attached, depending on the fabric weight or thickness (lighter fabrics can be gathered more). The depth of the ruffle will depend on the application: for children's clothes a small 1–3in (2.5–7.5cm) ruffle is sufficient; for adult hems, cuffs or neck edges, 4–8in (10–20cm) will be more suitable.

1 To create a ruffle, first hem one long edge and then gather the top edge as for gathering.

2 Set aside the ruffle and neaten the garment hem by turning up and pressing the hem allowance and trimming it to 1in (2.5cm).

3 With the garment and the ruffle right side uppermost, tuck the top edge of the ruffle under the garment hem edge so the raw edges match and pin the layers together.

4 Edge stitch close to the garment hem edge, catching the ruffle in place as you stitch.

5 Finish by neatening the raw edges of both ruffle and hem allowance with overcast stitch, overlocking, pinking shears or binding.

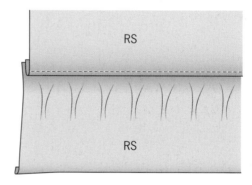

FIGURE 31 ATTACH THE RUFFLE BY EDGE STITCHING IT TO THE MAIN GARMENT PIECE.

LAPPED RUFFLE

A lapped ruffle is neatened top and bottom before gathering and stitching on top of the main garment fabric, overlapping the garment hem edge by 1in (2.5cm). It's also a very useful way to lengthen a garment that is too short.

SERGER TECHNIQUES

Sergers are very useful to have in addition to a regular sewing machine. As well as overlocking seam edges to neaten them, they can be used for hemming and for decorative surface treatments such as flat locking.

STARTING TO STITCH

1 Unlike using a sewing machine, you can start stitching on an overlocker with the presser foot down. Start by stitching a chain of about 4in (10cm).

2 Then introduce the fabric, guiding it so that the seam allowance is trimmed just prior to stitching; there will be markings on the side of the machine to show how far ⅝in (1.5cm) is from the needles.

3 At the end of a seam, continue stitching for a further 4in (10cm) and then feed the chain of stitches back through the overlocked seam or trim it off and dab it with fabric adhesive to prevent it unravelling.

OVERLOCKING

The most regularly used stitch on an serger is the overlock stitch, which, on a four-thread machine, can be used to stitch, cut and overcast the seam allowance all in one go. Three-thread overlocking will just finish the seam edge by trimming the fabric and overcasting at the same time. This can also be done with a four-thread serger by removing the left needle, setting the stitch width to the narrowest (usually 5) and the stitch length to 2.5. The looper should interlock on the fabric edge, so adjust the tensions a little at a time if this is not the case.

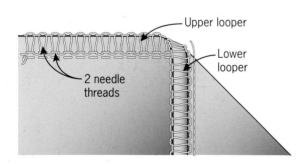

FIGURE 32 OVERLOCK SEAM ALLOWANCES TO STITCH, CUT AND OVERCAST THEM.

EXPERT TIP

To ensure that it doesn't fall into the throat plate, remove the needle before cutting the thread and tape it to the front of the machine for safe keeping. Always tighten the needle screw even when the needle is removed so the screw cannot work loose.

ROLLING HEMS

This is another technique for which the serger is perfect as it produces a very neat finish to the hem edge. It is particularly useful for transparent and lightweight fabrics where a turned-up hem allowance would be visible. As you stitch, the fabric edge is rolled under and caught within the loopers. It is stitched with a three-thread overlock stitch, so if you are working with a four-thread machine, remove the left needle, set the stitch length to 2 and remove the stitch finger (refer to your user manual as you may also need to change the throat plate and foot). Set the stitch width to medium and loosen the upper looper by one number and the lower looper by two (the tensions should be approximately 4, 4, 3, 6). (On some machines you may use the right needle not the left, so check the user manual.)

FLATLOCKING

The flatlock stitch is often used as a decorative surface treatment and will also make a hem with the stitching visible on the right side of the fabric.

1 To flatlock as a decorative detail, remove the right needle and ensure the stitch finger is in the working position. Set the left needle tension to 0, the stitch length to 2.5–3 and the width to the widest possible. Disengage the knife and fold the fabric with right sides out.

2 Stitch along the fold so the stitches appear to be loose along one side.

3 Once stitched, open out the fabric to flatten the stitching. The stitching creates a ladder appearance on the back although, if the fabric is folded right sides together before stitching, it will be on the front.

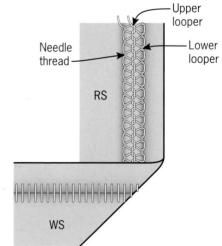

FIGURE 33 USE FLATLOCKING TO PRODUCE A DECORATIVE INSET.

For hemming, re-engage the knife. Then fold up a double hem so that it is 1in (2.5cm) shorter than required. Working from the right side, flatlock along the outer edge, cutting the fabric edge as you sew. Open out the fold to flatten the flatlocking on the surface.

OVERLOCKING IS OFTEN EASIEST ON LONG, STRAIGHT SEAMS, AS ON A PAIR OF TROUSERS.
THE TECHNIQUE IS ALSO PARTICULARLY GOOD FOR SEWING JERSEY/KNIT FABRICS.

UNDERSTANDING PAPER PATTERNS

THERE ARE LITERALLY HUNDREDS OF DESIGNS IN THE PATTERN COLLECTIONS OF ALL THE MAJOR PATTERN BRANDS — IN FACT SOMETHING TO SUIT EVERY SEWING NEED! THIS WIDE CHOICE OF PATTERNS CAN BE EXCITING OR DAUNTING, DEPENDING ON YOUR SEWING EXPERTISE. TO SIMPLIFY THE CHOICE, KEEP THREE CRITERIA IN MIND: LOOK FOR DESIGN DETAILS THAT YOU CAN SEW CONFIDENTLY. CHOOSE A STYLE YOU LIKE AND CHOOSE A STYLE THAT FLATTERS YOU.

CHOOSING THE PATTERN SIZE

All the major pattern brands use standard body measurements and a common international sizing guide. However, pattern sizing does differ from ready-to-wear, so it is very important to take accurate measurements before cutting into the tissue and fabric. Generally, you will probably be a larger pattern size than high street dress size because high street stores often use 'vanity sizing'.

In addition to the standard body measurements for misses' patterns shown below, the pattern brands publish body measurement charts for more mature women, as well as children and men, which you will find on their websites and on the back of relevant pattern envelopes.

Misses' Body Measurement Chart

Misses' patterns are designed for a well proportioned, developed figure, about 5'5" to 5'6" (1.65–1.68m) tall, without shoes

Size	4 (30)	6 (32)	8 (34)	10 (36)	12 (38)	14 (40)	16 (42)	18 (44)	20 (46)	22 (48)	24 (50)	26 (52)
Bust	29½ (75cm)	30½ (78cm)	31½ (80cm)	32½ (83cm)	34 (87cm)	36 (92cm)	38 (97cm)	40 (102cm)	42 (107cm)	44 (112cm)	46 (117cm)	48 (122cm)
Waist	22 (56cm)	23 (58cm)	24 (61cm)	25 (64cm)	26½ (67cm)	28 (71cm)	30 (76cm)	32 (81cm)	34 (87cm)	37 (94cm)	39 (99cm)	41½ (106cm)
Hip	31½ (80cm)	32½ (83cm)	32½ (85cm)	34½ (88cm)	36 (92cm)	38 (97cm)	40 (102cm)	44 (107cm)	44 (112cm)	46 (117cm)	48 (122cm)	50 (127cm)
Back waist length	15½ (38.5cm)	15½ (39.5cm)	15¾ (40cm)	16 (40.5cm)	16¼ (41.5cm)	16½ (42cm)	16¾ (42.5cm)	17¼ (43cm)	17¼ (44cm)	17⅜ (44cm)	17½ (44.5cm)	17¾ (44.5cm)

TAKING MEASUREMENTS

If possible, enlist a friend to help you take your measurements. Wear regular underwear and a close fitting top or dress.

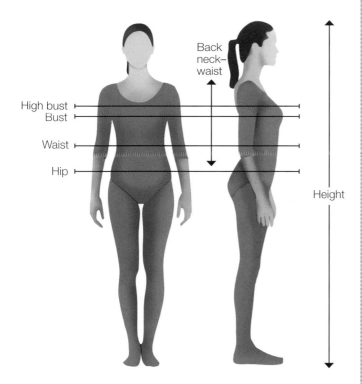

FIGURE 1 MEASURE THE SIX CRITICAL MEASUREMENTS SHOWN HERE.

Bust Measure with the tape straight across your back and the fullest part of your bust. Patterns are designed for a B cup, so if you are a C cup or more, you will also need to take the high bust measurement.

High bust/chest Measure straight across the back under the arms and above the bust at the front. If you are a C cup or more, use this measurement to choose your pattern when making a top, jacket, coat or dress.

Waist Tie a length of string or elastic round your waist and bend from side to side so that it settles on your natural waist before taking the measurement at the same point.

Hip Measure around the widest area of your hip, usually 7–9in (18–23 cm) below the natural waist.

Back neck-waist length Measure from the most prominent bone at the back of the neck to the natural waist.

Height Measure from the top of the head to the floor. This will help determine whether you are 'standard' size (height 5ft 6in (1.68m), or need a 'Fit for Petite' pattern designed for women of 5ft 4in (1.63m).

To determine your pattern size, compare your measurements with the pattern sizing on the back of the pattern envelope (see chart, p. 36). If you fall between two sizes, choose the smaller size if small boned and the larger size if big boned. For tops, jackets and dresses, choose by bust or high bust measurement. For skirts, trousers and shorts, choose the pattern size by waist measurement unless your hips are two pattern sizes or more larger than your waist pattern size. In that case, add 5in (13cm) to that measurement to determine the cup size.

FITTING EASE

Having determined your pattern size, next consider the fit of the garment. Every garment includes some wearing ease to allow movement ('wriggle room') and an element of 'design ease'. The amount of design ease depends entirely on how loose or close fitting the designer envisaged the style. Close-fitting garments include those with a boned bodice, a dress or jacket might be semi-fitted, and many coats are loose fitting. Many patterns list the actual garment measurements on the back of the envelope (or on the tissue pieces), which include body measurements, wearing ease and design ease.

A close-fitting garment, such as a stretch swimsuit or leotard, can be ½in (1.3cm) smaller than your actual body measurements or, alternatively, include just ½–1in (1.3–2.5cm) ease. Patterns designed for stretch knit fabrics also include less wearing ease as they will stretch over the body. On the other hand, a loose-fitting garment such as a coat, which is designed to be worn over a jacket, will have as much as 10in (2.5cm) wearing ease as well as some design ease.

DETERMINING CUP SIZE

To determine your bust cup size, take the bust and high bust measurement. The high bust measurement is the band measurement. If it is an odd number or part number, round it up to nearest even number. The difference between the two measurements is the cup size.

Cup size	Difference
A	1in (2.5cm)
B	2–2½in (5–6.5cm)
C	3–3½in (7.5–9cm)
D	4–4½in (10–11.5cm)
DD or E	5–5½in (13–14cm)
F	6in (15.5cm)
G	7in (18cm)

Alternatively, you can measure under the bust for the band measurement. In that case, add 5in (13cm) to that measurement to determine the cup size.

MAKING BASIC ADJUSTMENTS

If you are not the standard height or have a bust size over B cup, you will need to make a few basic adjustments to the pattern before cutting it out in fabric.

The correct length can make all the difference to how a garment looks. If sleeves are too long, a jacket will look too big, even though just shortening the sleeves will address the problem. If the crotch depth is too short, trousers will be uncomfortable; if it's too long, they will look baggy. Tops that have a waistline should be checked to ensure the tissue waistline is in the right place for you. If not, you will forever be pulling the top down. Most patterns have a lengthening and shortening line across the pieces.

To make bust adjustments on a pattern successfully, preferably chose a design with bust darts or princess seams (from the shoulder or armhole down over the bust). For princess seams, simply cut the tissue wider by the appropriate amount at the fullest part of the bust, tapering back to the original line above and below.

ENLARGING DARTS FOR A FULLER BUST

To decide whether you need to enlarge the darts, first determine your cup size by subtracting the high bust measurement from the bust measurement. If the difference is less than 2½in (6.5cm), you are an A–B cup and you will not need to alter the pattern. If it is 2½- 3in (6.5–7.5cm), you are C cup. If the difference is 3½–4in (9–10cm), you are a D cup and if 4in (10cm) or more, you are larger than a D cup.

1 Stick a piece of transparent tape over the bust point to strengthen the tissue.

2 Draw a line from the bust point diagonally up to the armhole notch (A). Continue this line, parallel to the centre front from the bust point down to the lower edge of the pattern (B). Draw another line from the centre of the existing underarm dart to the bust point (C).

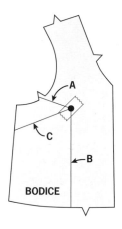

FIGURE 3 DRAW THREE LINES FROM THE BUST POINT TO: THE ARMHOLE NOTCH, THE LOWER EDGE AND THE CENTRE OF THE EXISTING DART.

3 Cut along lines A and B from the bottom edge, through the bust point to the armhole, but not through the armhole seam. Also cut along line C from the side edge towards, but not through, the bust point.

4 Place a spare piece of tissue under the cut edges and pin it in place between the centre front and cut line B. Then spread the tissue apart, keeping the cut edges parallel below the bust point. Spread the tissue apart, at the outer end of lines B and C, by ½in (1.3cm) for a C cup, ¾in (2cm) for a D cup and 1¼in (3cm) for larger than a D cup.

5 Tape all the cut edges in place on the underlying tissue. Then redraw the centre front lower edge to make it even with the bottom edge of the side bodice. Mark a new bust point 1–1¼in (2.5–3cm) closer to the side seam, but at same level, and draw new dart lines for the side to bust dart.

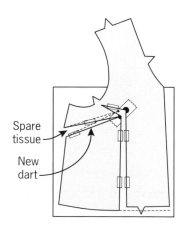

FIGURE 4 CUT ALONG THE LINES, BUT NOT THROUGH THE BUST POINT ON LINE C OR THE ARMHOLE SEAM.

Spare tissue

New dart

6 Pin the dart and fold it downwards. Then draw a new side seam line from the centre of the dart down to the original seam.

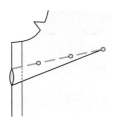

FIGURE 5 PIN THE DART IN ORDER TO DRAW A NEW SIDE SEAM.

CHANGING THE BUST DART POSITION

Sometimes the position of the bust dart on the pattern will not correspond to your own bust point. To check, first measure from the centre of your shoulder directly down to the fullest part of the bust. Compare this measurement with the same distance on the tissue, taken from the stitching line at the shoulder to the bust point. If the measurements are not the same, the bust dart position needs to be moved.

1 Mark the new bust point on the original tissue.

2 Next trace the original dart lines and bust point onto a spare piece of tissue paper.

3 Tape the traced dart over the original tissue, but so that the original bust point matches the new bust point. Redraw the side cutting lines.

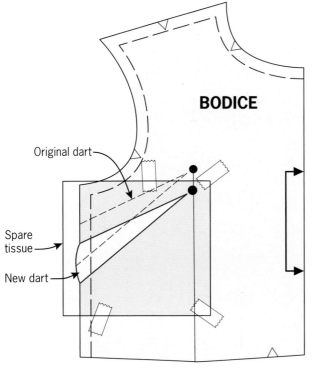

FIGURE 6 TRACE THE DART LINES AND REDRAW THE SIDE CUTTING LINES FOR THE CHANGED BUST DART POSITION.

MAKING MINOR WAIST AND HIP ADJUSTMENTS

Minor adjustments of 2in (5cm) or less to increase or decrease sizing at the waist or hip can simply be done by adding or subtracting a quarter of the amount to the side seam of the front and back pattern pieces.

1 Mark the new cutting line inside the original to decrease the sizing or outside the original, on spare tissue paper, to increase the sizing. Taper the new cutting line back to the original.

2 Then add the additional amount needed at the waist (if applicable) to the waistband or facings.

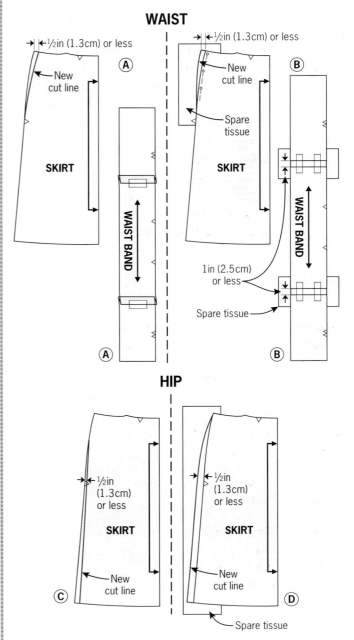

FIGURE 7 MAKE ADJUSTMENTS OF 2IN (5CM) OR LESS AT THE WAIST OR HIP: A) DECREASING AT THE WAIST. B) INCREASING AT THE WAIST. C) DECREASING AT THE HIP. D) INCREASING AT THE HIP.

MAKING MAJOR WAIST AND HIP ADJUSTMENTS

Before increasing a pattern at the waist or hip by more than 2in (5cm), consider whether cutting a larger size pattern would be a better option. If not, avoid distorting the design line by making the alterations down the middle of the pattern pieces.

1 Slash the pattern front and back pieces down the middle, spreading them by a quarter of the total amount to be added and taping a new piece of tissue piece in place.

2 If it is necessary to add a waist dart, because the increase is just for the hip area, fold out each of the four darts (two at the front and two at the back) a quarter of the total amount to be reduced. The dart should be approximately 5in (13cm) long tapering to nothing above the hip.

3 Add the total adjustment to the waistband or facings as shown in Figure 9.

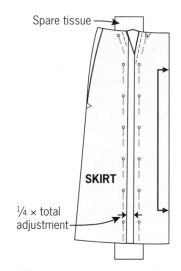

FIGURE 8 MAKE ADJUSTMENTS OF MORE THAN 2IN (5CM) DOWN THE MIDDLE OF THE PATTERN PIECES, ADDING FURTHER ADJUSTMENTS AT THE WAIST AFTER ACCOMMODATING THE HIPS.

SHORTENING A BODICE

First identify the lengthening and shortening line on the pattern pieces and then follow the steps below. However, if the pattern doesn't have a lengthening and shortening line, and the adjustment is just a few inches, simply cut it from the bottom.

1 Mark the amount the bodice needs to be shortened by and draw a line across the pattern above the printed line.

2 Then fold the pattern along the printed line and bring it up to the new line, taping it in place.

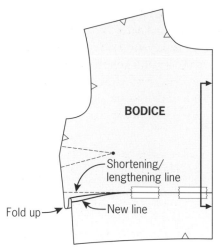

FIGURE 9 FOLD THE PRINTED LINE UP TO THE NEW LINE TO SHORTEN THE BODICE.

3 Redraw the side cutting lines, seams and darts as necessary. Repeat on all the bodice pieces.

LENGTHENING A BODICE

As with making any adjustments, measure yourself first and compare the measurements with the tissue pattern.

1 Cut the pattern piece along the lengthening and shortening line.

2 Spread the tissue apart by the required amount and tape it to a spare piece of tissue.

3 Redraw any side cutting lines, seams and darts as necessary. Repeat on all the bodice pieces.

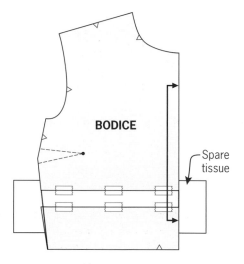

FIGURE 10 CUT THE PATTERN PIECE AND ADD THE APPROPRIATE AMOUNT TO LENGTHEN THE BODICE.

ADJUSTING TROUSERS

Trousers should fit smoothly over the hips and bottom. They should also be comfortable enough for you to sit, move and bend easily. If they are too tight in the crotch area, they may wrinkle upwards. If they are too loose, wrinkles may radiate downwards. To make pattern adjustments, first measure yourself and then compare the measurements with the tissue piece.

1 The crotch depth is measured from the waist to the crotch seam. To take the measurement, sit up straight on a dining chair and measure from your waist to the seat and then add ½in (1.3cm) ease for hips up to 36in (91.5cm) or 1¼in (3cm) for larger hips.

2 On the pattern tissue, draw a line from the crotch seam across to the side seam. Measure down the side seam to the drawn crotch line and compare this with your body measurement.

3 If the crotch depth needs to be shortened or lengthened, fold up the tissue or cut it apart on the lengthening and shortening line as for a skirt.

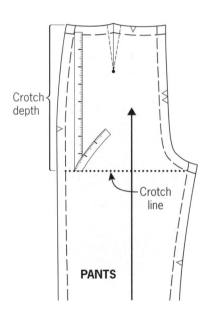

FIGURE 11 COMPARE YOUR OWN BODY MEASUREMENT WITH THE CROTCH DEPTH ON THE PATTERN.

4 Then check the crotch length. With a tape measure standing on its side on the pattern pieces, measure from the front waist seam to the inner crotch seam. Then repeat from the back waist seam to the inner leg seam again. Add these measurements together.

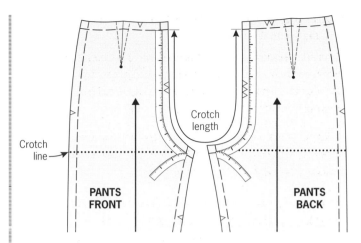

FIGURE 12 MEASURE THE CROTCH LENGTH ON THE PAPER PATTERN.

5 Now take your own body measurements from the front waist and under the crotch to the back waist, adding 1½–2in (4–5cm) for ease.

6 Compare the measurements. If you need to adjust the tissue, first check whether you should do this equally on both front and back pieces or whether you have a larger derrière or rounded tummy. Divide the appropriate amount either equally or proportionally depending on your figure shape. Add or subtract the measurement to the inner leg seam on each pattern piece.

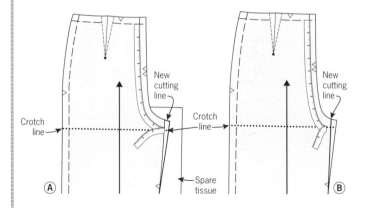

FIGURE 13 TO LENGTHEN OR SHORTEN THE CROTCH LENGTH, ADD (A) OR SUBTRACT (B) FROM THE INNER LEG SEAM.

WHAT'S IN A PATTERN

A pattern is more than a bag of tissue pieces – it includes everything you need to know to make up the design from fabric choice and amount to helpful sewing tips to see you through to completion, as well as garment measurements and sizing guidelines.

PATTERN ENVELOPE

The front of the pattern envelope shows not only images of the designs included in the pack but also logos noting whether the design is easy to sew or a 'timed' design, the design number and the sizes included in the pack.

There is also a wealth of information on the back of the pattern envelope, including:

Line drawings show the design details such as seam lines, dart placement, type of waistband and other features, zipper and pocket placement, etc.

Number of pieces give an indication of how easy the pattern will be to make up.

Suggested fabrics list all the fabrics that are known to work well for the design.

Sizing guidelines. Choose your size according to the garment type (see p. 37).

Fabric requirements give the amount of fabric needed to make each item, which may include a 'with nap' or 'without nap' requirement (see p. 45).

Notions are listed as required for each garment style.

Garment measurements comprise of body measurements, wearing ease and design ease.

FIGURE 14 THE FRONT OF THE PATTERN ENVELOPE GIVES YOU VARIOUS PIECES OF INFORMATION AS WELL AS THE MAIN FEATURES OF THE DESIGN.

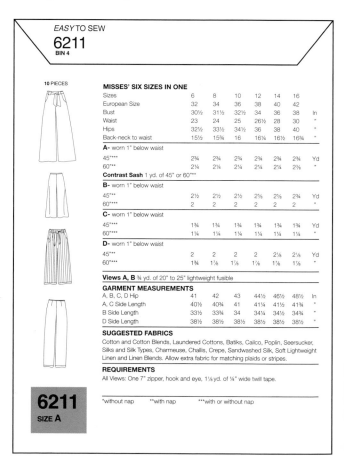

FIGURE 15 THE BACK OF THE PATTERN ENVELOPE GIVES LOTS OF INFORMATION. FOR CLARITY ONLY IMPERIAL MEASUREMENTS ARE GIVEN HERE; COMMERCIAL PATTERNS ALSO GIVE METRIC MEASUREMENTS.

PATTERN INSTRUCTION SHEETS

There are instruction sheets inside the pattern pack that include not only the step-by-step construction notes, but also layouts for fabric and other useful information, including:

Garment illustrations show all the variations included in the pack.

Garment pieces, numbered and listed, show which pieces you need for each garment.

Cutting layouts for each garment show how to lay out the pattern pieces on the main and fabrics, and interfacing.

General sewing directions and advice on how to use the pattern help you to construct the garment easily.

PATTERN MARKINGS AND NOTCHES

More helpful information is printed on each of the pattern tissue pieces, including the number of pieces to cut, how to lay them on the fabric and any placement marks for buttonholes, darts or pockets that need to be transferred to the fabric.

Seam allowances are included (although not always shown) on all the well-known commercial patterns – usually $\frac{5}{8}$in (1.5cm) on dressmaking patterns. On multi-size patterns, cutting lines common to all sizes are shown as solid lines, whereas those for each different size are shown with a different type of line.

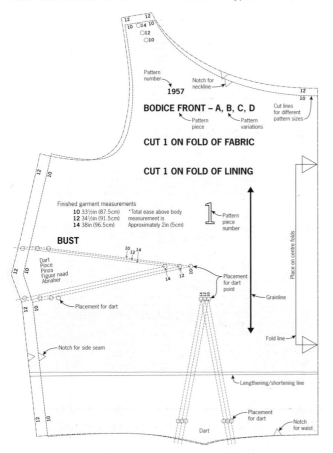

FIGURE 16 MAKE SURE YOU UNDERSTAND THE INFORMATION ON THE PATTERN PIECES BEFORE YOU CUT OUT THEM OR THE FABRIC.

The information on the pattern pieces includes:

Notches are the triangular marks on the cutting line around the edge of the pattern piece. They are used to match corresponding pieces on sleeves and armholes, collars and neck edges or facings and front edges.

Circular markings indicate the placement of features such as darts, pockets, zippers, facings, etc.

The **grainline** is shown by a thick straight line, usually with arrowheads at each end. Make sure this line runs parallel with the fabric grainline (selvage) to ensure that the drape of the finished garment is correct.

Foldline Some pattern pieces should be placed on a fold of fabric to cut two symmetrical halves at once. The foldline is indicated by a line with arrowheads at right angles at each end. Place the foldline against the fold of the fabric, having folded the fabric so the selvages match.

Lengthening and shortening line indicates where the pattern can be lengthened or shortened without spoiling the finished design.

Placements for darts, tucks, pleats and buttonholes are shown by dotted or dashed lines. Pleats and tucks may also have directional arrows between the lines indicating which way to fold the fabric to form the pleat.

Finished garment measurements may be listed for each size at key fitting areas.

EXPERT TIP

Identify the fabric layout that suits your fabric and circle it with a pen so you don't accidentally start following another layout if you get interrupted.

CUTTING OUT THE FABRIC

The pattern instruction sheet shows how to fold the fabric ready to lay out the pattern pieces. Generally the fabric is folded, right sides together, with the selvages parallel to each other.

1 Pin the pattern pieces in place and then double check that they are correctly laid out against the appropriate layout on the pattern instruction sheet.

2 Cut out the fabric carefully, following the cut lines for your size and using sharp, good quality dressmaking shears. Cut out around the notches rather than into the seam allowance.

3 Transfer any markings on the pattern tissue to the fabric with a chalk pencil or marking pen. If it is difficult to tell the right from the wrong side of the fabric, mark the wrong side on all the pieces with a chalk cross to ensure you always put pieces together correctly.

EXPLORING FABRICS

THERE ARE MANY FABRICS SUITABLE FOR DIFFERENT STYLES AND GARMENTS. MANY ARE EASY TO WORK WITH, BUT IF YOU CHOOSE DELICATE, NOVELTY AND HEAVYWEIGHT FABRICS, YOU WILL ALSO NEED TO CONSIDER SPECIAL SEWING TECHNIQUES. CHOOSING THE RIGHT TYPE OF FABRIC CAN MAKE ALL THE DIFFERENCE BETWEEN A GARMENT THAT LOOKS GREAT AND ONE THAT DOES NOT!

GENERAL FABRIC KNOW-HOW

It is useful to know several terms associated with fabric, as listed below.

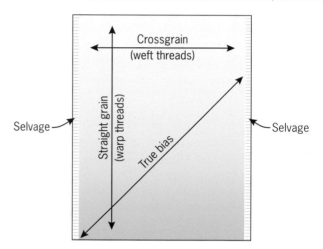

FIGURE 1 FABRIC STRETCHES LEAST ALONG THE STRAIGHT GRAIN AND MOST ACROSS THE BIAS.

GRAIN

All woven fabrics have weft and warp threads, which give them a grain. Weft threads go across the fabric from side to side, giving the crossgrain (crosswise grain). Warp threads run lengthways down the fabric and parallel to the selvages. The warp threads create the straight (lengthwise) grain, which is the most stable. Most pattern pieces are therefore laid out along the straight grain.

BIAS

The fabric bias is a line across the fabric in any diagonal direction. However, the true bias is at 45-degrees to the selvage. To find the true bias, simply fold the cut edge of fabric up to one selvage. The fold is on the true bias. The true bias has the greatest stretch.

SELVAGE

There are two selvages on a length of fabric, down the side edges. They are often slightly more tightly woven than the rest of the fabric, so it is advisable to cut the selvages off before sewing seams. If they are used in a seam allowance, snip into the allowance every few inches to release some of the woven tension.

NAP

Fabrics that have a pile surface have 'nap'. These include velvet, fleece, faux fur, etc. The nap causes shading when the fabric is brushed one way or another, and so all pieces of a garment should be laid on the fabric in the same direction from top to bottom. Similarly, fabrics with a one-way design on them, including checks and plaids, should be treated as if they have a nap and all pattern pieces laid in the same direction to match the fabric design. More fabric is needed to follow 'with nap' layouts.

CUTTING OUT TIPS

- Fold the fabric as advised by the pattern; this is usually right sides together with the selvages parallel. Speciality fabrics, checks and plaids are best cut from a single layer of fabric, right side up, so that the pattern pieces can be placed side by side to ensure that notches and other balance marks, such as darts and waist line, match up in relation to the fabric design.

- Take care when placing the pattern pieces on checked or striped fabric. Make sure that wide stripes do not run across the widest part of the body.

- If pattern pieces have a straight grainline, ensure this is parallel to the selvage. Fabric cut off grain will have more stretch, causing seams to ripple and pucker. Check each pattern piece is laying along the straight grain by measuring from the selvage straight across to both the top and bottom of the printed grainline. Adjust the position if necessary before pinning the pattern in place.

- Pin the tissue to the fabric following the pattern layout, pinning only within the seam allowance. If working with fabrics that shouldn't be pinned, such as PVC, vinyl, faux leather or suede, use fabric weights or tins of food.

- Use sharp dressmaking shears to cut out the fabric.

- Transfer the markings for darts, pleats, tucks, zippers, pockets, buttons, etc. from the tissue to the fabric (see pp. 8–9 for a choice of tools).

- Garment sections cut on the bias need to be stabilized in areas where stretch is not wanted, such as around the neckline, armholes and shoulders, before seaming. Use stay stitch (see p. 25) or edge tape in the seam allowance.

- Cut out interfacing at the same time as fabric. Press it into place on relevant pieces so they are ready to use as needed.

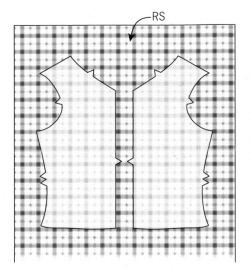

FIGURE 2 WHEN WORKING WITH CHECKS AND PLAIDS, POSITION THE PATTERN PIECES SO THAT NOTCHES AND BALANCE MARKS MATCH UP IN RELATION TO THE FABRIC DESIGN.

SEWING SENSE

After unpinning the pattern pieces, keep them with the fabric for easy reference when making up.

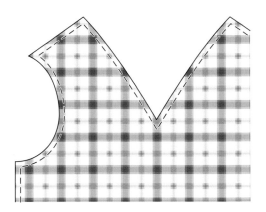

FIGURE 3 STAY STITCH SECTIONS THAT NEED TO BE STABILIZED SO THEY DO NOT STRETCH.

FABRIC CHOICES

Commercial patterns usually list suggested fabrics for the garment design on the back of the pattern envelope. However, it is always useful to know what the different types of fabric are and how to sew them for the best results. Here is a listing of the most commonly used fabrics for dressmaking.

VERY LIGHTWEIGHT CHIFFON, GEORGETTE, ORGANZA

Garments These fabrics are suitable for tops, over-skirts, over-dresses and scarves.

Properties Very lightweight and transparent, these woven fabrics can be more difficult to sew as they are very fluid and slippery. Often mixed with synthetic fibres, they can be crease-resistant. They are very delicate, however, and must be handled with care to prevent snagging. Organza has a crisper handle, while georgette is slight more opaque than chiffon.

Needles and stitch length 60–70 (9–10) sharps or general-purpose needles and stitch length 2–2.2 are recommended.

Thread Silk thread is preferable because it is softer on the fabric. However, general-purpose polyester-covered cotton is also acceptable.

Interfacing Use lightweight fusible interfacing or self-interface with the same fabric. Use soluble or tearaway stabilizer behind buttonholes when stitching, removing it afterwards.

Seams and neatening methods French seams are best on straight edges (see p. 27), while a double stitched seam is also ideal (see p. 27). Hems can be bound or rolled. Pin frequently to hold flimsy fabrics together and use sharp, serrated shears to grip the fabric as you cut it out. If possible, use a straight stitch throat plate that has only a tiny hole for the needle, thus preventing the delicate fabric being pulled into the feed dogs. If seams pucker, add a layer of tissue paper or soluble stabilizer under or on top of the seam line and remove it once the seam is stitched.

Similar fabrics include muslins, voiles, handkerchief linen, gauze and organdie.

LIGHTWEIGHT COTTONS, COTTON BLENDS, LINENS, LINEN BLENDS, POLY/COTTONS, POPLINS

Garments These fabrics are suitable for lightweight summer clothes, dresses, tops and trousers.

Properties They are all stable, woven fabrics, easy to sew, neaten and press, so are very suitable for novice sewers. Cotton comes from cotton plants, while linen comes from flax. As natural fabrics, they will 'breathe' more easily, but do tend to crease. Mixed with synthetic fibres, they have greater strength and crease-resistant properties. Both cotton and linen are available as very lightweight fabrics or can be heavier weight for shift dresses and jackets.

Needles and stitch length 70–80 (10–12) sharps or general-purpose needles and stitch length 2.2–2.5 are recommended.

Thread General-purpose threads, such as polyester-covered cottons work well.

Interfacing Lightweight fusible or sew-in interfacing can be used. If using fusible interfacing, trim the edges so that it sits just inside the seam line.

Seams and neatening methods Lightweight stable fabrics can be seamed with regular straight seams and neatened with pinking shears for a quick-fix solution. Alternatives include zigzag or overcast stitching seam allowances together, then trimming close to the stitching. French seams also work well (see p. 27).

Similar fabrics include cotton lawn, cotton batiste, gingham, broadcloth, broderie anglais (eyelet embroidery), calico, chambray, cheesecloth and seersucker.

MEDIUM-WEIGHT COTTONS, COTTON MIXES, DENIM

Garments These fabrics are suitable for skirts, structured tops, jackets and trousers.

Properties They have the same properties as lightweight cottons, but with some weight, making them suitable for more structured garments.

Needles and stitch length 75–80 (11–12) general-purpose needles are recommended or, for denim, use a jeans needle. Use stitch length 2.5–3, depending on the number of fabric layers.

Thread Cotton or polyester-covered cotton work well.

Interfacing Use medium-weight fusible or sew-in interfacing.

Seams and neatening methods Regular straight seams can be used, or try welt or flat fell seams when seaming is part of the detail or to encase the raw edges of seam allowances. Grade the seam allowances to reduce bulk in the seams (see p. 26).

Similar fabrics include drill, twill, sail cloth, canvas, chintz, damask and brocade.

SEWING SENSE
Denim is a lovely fabric to work with, but can be medium- or heavyweight and very crisp. Decide which weight to use for a garment by holding a length of fabric to check how it handles and see how it falls, pleats, folds and creases.

SILK, SATIN, SATEEN, CRÈPE DE CHINE, POLYESTER, VISCOSE

Garments Silky fabrics can range from light- to heavyweight so can be used for all sorts of dressmaking. Satin and sateens are particularly good for bridal and evening wear, ball gowns and bustiers. Silks and crèpe de chine are good for dresses, tops and flowing A-line skirts.

Properties These woven fabrics need delicate handling as they fray and mark easily, and can snag if needles are blunt or hands are rough. Pin them only within the seam allowances. Press them on a silk setting and always use a press cloth. When using fabrics with a sheen, such as satins and silks, follow the 'with nap' layout and lay all the pattern pieces on the fabric in the same direction so that any shading is the same throughout.

Needles and stitch length Use 70–80 (10–12) fine, sharp needles and 2.2–2.5 stitch length.

Thread Preferably use silk thread with silk fabrics, although general-purpose polyester-covered cottons also work well.

Interfacing Soft woven interfacings work best. Fusibles can be used, but press carefully, always using a press cloth. Use lightweight interfacings with lightweight fabrics and medium-weight with heavier weight satins and sateens.

Seams and neatening methods Regular straight stitch seams or French seams work well. Neaten raw edges well, with overlock, overcast or Hong Kong finish (see p. 28). When stitching bias-cut seams, slightly stretch the seam behind and in front of the needle as you sew. Once pressed, it will relax into a straight seam without ripples.

Similar fabrics include rayon, acetate, china silk and Thai silk (both used for linings), cire, dupion, shantang, charmeuse, shantung, raw silk, silk noil, sueded silk, sandwashed silk, duchesse satin, satin-backed crepe/crepe-backed satin, taffeta and faille.

SEWING SENSE
Treat fabrics with a sheen or satin finish as if they have nap as they may reflect the light differently when held one way or another.

LIGHTWEIGHT WOOLS, GABARDINE, FLANNEL, WOOL CREPE

Garments These fabrics suit structured garments such as trousers, jackets, fitted dresses and straight skirts. It is best to line them to prevent 'seating' and to keep the garment in good condition.

Properties These are stable, woven fabrics which respond well to shaping with steam. Pure wool is a natural cloth and therefore breathes well. Take care when pressing, using a press cloth, and allow the fabric to cool completely when using steam to prevent unwanted stretching. Different weaves provide a different textural surface, such as twill, herringbone, faille and jacquard.

Needles and stitch length Use 80–90 (12–14) universal needles and 2.5–3 mm stitch length, depending on the number of fabric layers being stitched.

Thread Use general-purpose polyester or polyester-covered cotton. Thicker buttonhole or top-stitch thread should be used for buttonholes and top stitching.

Interfacings Use woven, light- to medium-weight interfacings. Build up layers in key areas on jackets and coats to add support and maintain shaping (see pp. 124–125 on speed tailoring).

Seams and neatening methods Regular straight seams, neatened with overcast or overlock stitch or Hong Kong finish (see p. 28) are recommended. Grade the seam allowances to reduce bulk (see p. 26) and understitch the facings (see p. 25).

Similar fabrics include herringbone, wool blends, woollen mixes.

MEDIUM- TO HEAVYWEIGHT WOOLS, TWEEDS, COATINGS, FLEECE

Garments These fabrics work well for coats, jackets, shawls, tops, gilets and suits. Medium-weight fabrics mould well and can be used for most structured garments. Heavier weight tweeds, coatings, etc. are bulky and so work best with minimal seaming and simple design lines. All these fabrics are best lined to prevent 'seating' and to maintain the garment in good condition.

Properties These range from matted fibres in coatings, to loose weave in tweeds and novelty tweeds. Handle them with care to prevent stretching and stay stitch all curved edges before sewing the seams. Some woollens have a soft sheen so use 'with nap' layouts.

Needles and stitch length Use 90–110 (14–18) universal or jeans needles for thicker fabrics. Use stitch length 3–3.5 or 3.5–5, depending on the fabric thickness and number of layers.

Thread General-purpose polyester or polyester-covered cotton work well. Use buttonhole thread or top-stitching thread for buttonholes.

Interfacings Use medium- to heavyweight fusible or sew-in interfacing. As with lightweight wools, build up layers when speed tailoring.

Seams and neatening methods Regular straight seams, neatened with overcast or overlock stitch or Hong Kong finish (see p. 28) are recommended. Lapped seams also work well on fleece and other woollens that do not fray (see p. 28). Grade all the seam allowances to reduce bulk (see p. 26) and understitch the facings (see p. 25).

Similar fabrics include corduroy, vicuna, worsted, serge, mohair, melton, loden, bouclé, cashmere, alpaca, angora and camel hair.

STRETCH KNITS, JERSEY, DOUBLE KNITS

Garments Choose patterns designed for stretch knit fabrics such as tops, pull-on dresses, skirts, elasticated-waist trousers and sports wear. Jersey fabrics are wonderful to work with as they are easy to fit, stretching over the body, and easy to sew using the correct needle and seaming.

Properties The fibres are knitted together rather than woven, providing stretch. Double-knit fabrics are double thickness. Other variations include ribbing. Knit fabrics can be silk, cotton or polyester, so pressing and handling will depend on the fabric type. For silk jersey, press on the silk setting and use a press cloth.

Needles and stitch length Use a ballpoint or stretch needle, size 75–90 (10–14), depending on fabric weight. Use a small zigzag stitch, length 2.5 and width 1.5–2.

Thread Polyester-covered cotton works best as it has some flexibility.

Interfacing Knit interfacings, which stretch with the fabric, can be fusible or sewn-in. Choose the weight to suit the fabric.

Seams and neatening Use stretch stitch or zigzag stitch to sew seams that need to have stretch in them. Stabilize neck edges and armholes before stitching, using stay stitch (see p. 25) in the seam allowance or edge tape. Pin carefully as blunt pins can cause snags or runs. Many knits do not need neatening as they do not fray. However, to prevent the raw edges curling, finish edges with overlock or zigzag stitch, and then trim the seam allowance close to stitching. When stitching bias-cut seams, slightly stretch the seam behind and in front of the needle as you sew. Once pressed, it will relax into a straight seam. Hem with top stitch or blind hem. Lettuce edge hemming also works well on stretch fabrics.

Similar fabrics include Lycra®, cotton knit, spandex, stretch velour.

VELVETS, FAUX FUR, FAUX SUEDE, LEATHER

Garments These fabrics work well for gilets, jackets, simple skirts, dresses and trousers.

Properties They have a pile or surface texture that changes when stroked one way or another, so use the 'with nap' layout. Some of these fabrics are woven, others knitted. Use double-sided tape or bulldog clips to temporarily hold seams together on faux suede and leather as pinning will mark them. Press with a dry iron and use either a velvet board or soft towel as a pressing surface, all to avoid flattening the pile.

Needles and stitch length Use size 80–90 (12–14) needles, universals for wovens and ball-points for knitted fabrics. For leathers and faux suede, use a leather needle with a specially shaped shaft. Stitch length will vary according to fabric thickness, but start with 2.5– 3.

Thread Use silk for silk velvets, or general-purpose polyester or polyester-covered cotton.

Interfacing Use sew-in interfacings, medium- or heavyweight to match the fabric weight. Trim the interfacing close to the seam line once it is sewn in place.

Seams and neatening methods Regular straight stitch seams work well. Alternatives include lapped and welt seams for non-fray fabrics. Velvet and faux fur fabrics can be difficult to sew as the piles rub together, causing the layers to 'walk'. Avoid this by using a walking foot that feeds both layers evenly. Grade seam allowances and trim off the pile in seam allowances to reduce bulk. Cut out heavily piled fabrics in a single layer and, working from the wrong side, cut just the backing, not the pile. Use a 'non-stitck' foot or roller foot on fabrics such as leather and pvc to help them feed evenly.

Similar fabrics include leatherette, leather, pvc, buckskin, chenille, panne velvet, velveteen and devoré.

SEWING SENSE
If a special presser foot isn't available, add a strip of tissue paper or soluble stabilizer to the seam line and tear it away after stitching. Alternatively, sprinkle a little talcum powder along the seam line.

SPECIALITY FABRICS, INCLUDING LACE, LAMÉ, SEQUINED AND BEADED FABRICS

Garments Use these luxury fabrics for accent pieces such as tops, bustiers, boleros, cropped jackets, shrugs and special occasion evening wear. Choose simple styles with few seams and design features.

Properties These fabrics can be made from silk, cotton or polyester and finished with surface embellishment such as beading, sequins sewn to a backing fabric, cording on lace or other raised embroideries. Follow 'with nap' layouts and use sharp shears to cut out the fabric. Fabrics that shimmer or change colour through the length are called iridescent, ombre or changeant. Cut facings from lining rather than the speciality fabric.

Needles and stitch length Use 70–80 (10–12) universal needles and stitch length 2.2–2.5. Change the needles more frequently than usual as the special finish on the fabric can blunt them more easily.

Threads Use silk for silk fabrics, otherwise use general-purpose polyester or polyester-coated cotton.

Interfacing Use sew-in interfacing of a weight to suit the fabric or use plain chiffon in a matching colour. Trim it close to the seam line once it is sewn in place.

Seams and neatening Cut out the pattern pieces from a single layer of fabric, right side up, turning each piece over to cut a right and left side. Use regular straight seams, but remove any beading or sequins from the seam line and seam allowance by carefully cutting away or crushing them (do not just cut the threads as more beading might unravel). If the beading is bulky, use a zipper foot to sew the seams. When sewing ombre fabrics, make sure the notches on the pattern pieces are in line with each other so the fabric shading matches across the pieces. Neaten the edges with Hong Kong finish or overcast stitch. Always use a press cloth when pressing. Avoid using steam on sequinned fabric.

Similar fabrics include Chantilly lace.

EXPERT TIP

The stitch length used will depend on the fabric weight, number of layers and stitch technique. For instance, for basting, use the longest stitch length; for ease stitching, slightly increase the length; and for sewing around corners, decrease the stitch length by 1 at each side of the corner. Always test stitch lengths of the same number of fabric and interfacing layers before committing to garment pieces.

WORKING WITH LACE

A garment made from an all-over lace fabric can look stunning, particularly if the seams appear to be invisible. This can be achieved by using a special lace seaming technique.

1 Cut out the pattern piece and lay it on a single layer of the fabric, with the seam line running through the centre of the lace motifs. Carefully mark the seam line on the fabric using a basting thread in a contrasting colour.

2 Now carefully take hand running stitches (thread trace) around the rest of the central lace motifs, outside the seam line, using a contrast colour of thread. Then cut out the garment piece, including cutting out around the lace design.

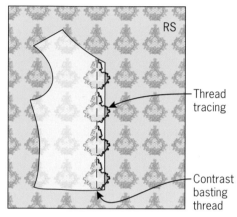

- Thread tracing
- Contrast basting thread

FIGURE 4 MARK THE SEAM LINE WITH BASTING STITCHES AND THREAD TRACE AROUND THE MOTIFS.

3 Flip the pattern piece, or lay the corresponding piece over the cut-out section, with the seam lines on top of each other. On the pattern, trace around the overlapping lace design, which was previously thread traced.

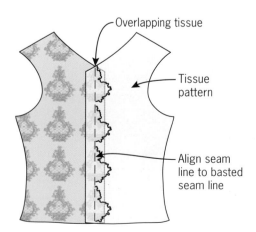

- Overlapping tissue
- Tissue pattern
- Align seam line to basted seam line

FIGURE 5 TRACE THE OVERLAPPING LACE MOTIFS ONTO THE PATTERN TISSUE.

4 Place the marked tissue piece on another single layer of lace fabric, positioning it so that the traced motifs on the tissue match up with the lace design on the fabric. Mark the seam line on the fabric and cut the piece out along the cutting line.

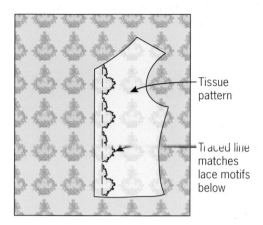

- Tissue pattern
- Traced line matches lace motifs below

FIGURE 6 POSITION THE PATTERN PIECE OVER THE LACE MOTIF AND MARK THE SEAM LINE BEFORE CUTTING OUT.

5 Lap the lace sections over each other, matching seam lines and motifs, with the cut-out motifs on the top. Baste around the overlapping motifs again and then machine stitch the layers together, carefully stitching around the edges of the overlapping motifs.

6 Using small sharp scissors, trim away the underlapping fabric close to the stitching. Press carefully.

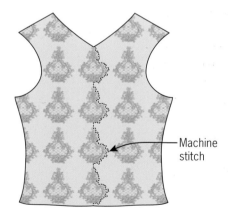

- Machine stitch

FIGURE 7 CAREFULLY TRIM THE EXCESS FABRIC CLOSE TO THE STITCHING.

USING INTERFACING, STABILIZER AND UNDERLINING

INTERFACING, UNDERLINING AND STABILIZER ARE SPECIAL FABRICS TO BE USED IN CONJUNCTION WITH THE MAIN FABRIC, EACH WITH A SPECIFIC PURPOSE. INTERFACING OR UNDERLINING IS OFTEN APPLIED TO HELP GIVE A GARMENT BODY AND STRUCTURE, AND MAINTAIN ITS SHAPE. STABILIZERS ARE USED TO PREVENT FABRIC PUCKERING IN HEAVILY STITCHED AREAS.

INTERFACING

Interfacing is sewn or fused to the reverse of the main fabric, primarily to support areas of strain, such as on facings or around buttonholes, or give structure to features like collars and cuffs. Without interfacing, the fabric would not retain its shape or hang properly and, in areas of dense stitching such as buttonholes, may pucker.

There are many different types of interfacing to suit different applications, fabric types and the effects you might wish to achieve. While there are no definitive rules, generally, the aim is to provide support without changing the handle of the main fabric. Therefore the weight of the interfacing should be the same as the main fabric: thus lightweight interfacing for lightweight fabric, etc. On very light, transparent fabrics the interfacing can simply be another layer of the main fabric.

Purpose-made interfacings can be divided into three categories:

Non-woven interfacing is the most commonly used and traditional. Primarily available in white or charcoal/black, it is made from pressed fibres to give a felt-like appearance. Thus pattern pieces can be placed in any direction to achieve an economical layout. It is available in fusible and sew-in varieties, and in different weights ranging from super-light to firm.

Woven interfacing is particularly useful when applied to a woven fabric that needs to have movement. Like fabric, it has a grain, which must be followed, and is also available in different weights. Colourways include skin tone, cream, white, charcoal and black. The lightweight skin tone variety is perfect when working with transparent fabrics such as chiffon or with lightweight silks and satins. The medium- and heavyweight varieties are used for dresses, jackets and blouses.

Knitted interfacing is fusible, flexible and stretches in the same way as knitted fabric. This makes it ideal for stretch knits. Colour choices include nude, white and charcoal.

It is quite conceivable that you might use a mixture of these interfacings in one garment. For instance, a stretch knit dress will have areas (such as the neckline) that shouldn't stretch where you might use a non-woven interfacing. Other areas that require support, but still need to stretch, would be better interfaced with a knitted variety.

Batting, also known as wadding or fleece, is a thicker, soft interfacing or interlining used to add bulk and warmth, particularly in quilting or for quilted jackets and coats. Often described as having extra loft (thickness), they can be plain white or have pre-printed quilting guidelines. A thermal wadding is more compressed to provide heat resistance.

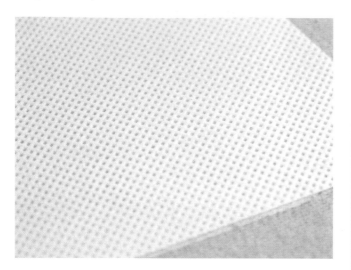

APPLYING FUSIBLE INTERFACING

Fusible interfacing is quicker to use than the sew-in type, but it is important to ensure it is fused completely and permanently otherwise the fabrics can ripple and bubble when laundered because the interfacing has come away from the main fabric. To ensure a firm hold take the following steps.

1 Cut out interfacing using the special pattern piece provided or the same pattern piece as the main fabric section. Trim the seam allowance from the edges of the interfacing so that it sits just within the seam line.

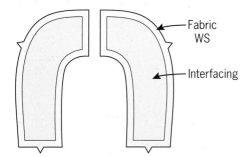

FIGURE 1 TRIM THE SEAM ALLOWANCE TO JUST WITHIN THE SEAM LINE.

2 Place the adhesive side of the interfacing, which has a slightly rough feel and a sheen, down on the wrong side of the fabric piece.

3 Cover with a press cloth and dry press with a medium to hot iron. Press rather than iron: place the iron on the covered interfacing, hold it in place for at least 10 seconds, then lift it and move to the next position. The time taken to fuse the interfacing in place will depend on the weight of the interfacing and the thickness and texture of the fabric. Check timings on a scrap of fabric before committing to the garment pieces.

4 Allow the garment piece to cool completely before continuing to sew.

EXPERT TIP

Use a press cloth such as organza, which can withstand hot temperatures and is transparent so you can see what you are pressing. Fuse all the sections to be interfaced in one go so they are ready to use when needed.

APPLYING SEW-IN INTERFACING

Sew-in interfacing is best for fabrics with surface detail, such as pile fabrics, like velvet and furs, or those with embellishments that might get damaged with heavy pressing.

1 Cut out the interfacing using the pattern piece as for fusibles.

2 Hand or machine stitch the interfacing to the wrong side of the fabric piece, stitching within the seam allowance, just outside seam line.

3 Trim away the excess interfacing close to the stitching. Trim the corners at an angle, again close to the stitching.

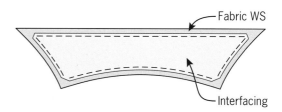

FIGURE 2 TRIM THE SEAM ALLOWANCE ON THE INTERFACING CLOSE TO THE STITCHING.

SPECIALIST INTERFACING PRODUCTS

As well as the regular interfacings, there are also specialist products to help provide support in specific areas. These include waistbanding and hemming tapes.

WAISTBANDING

Usually fusible and non-woven, this range includes slotted and stiffened banding, both of which help waistbands to retain their shape and firmness.

Slotted banding comes in different widths to suit different width waistbands, with a central row of slots between top and bottom rows. The slots allow the band to be folded easily and evenly without adding bulk at the fold, while retaining support from the interfacing.

FIGURE 3 FOLD SLOTTED BANDING TO SUPPORT A WAISTBAND.

Stiffened banding is approximately 1¼in (3cm) wide and provides a roll-resistant waistband interfacing. An alternative variety has a wider band, with a slotted line down the centre and an additional stiffened section covering half the banding.

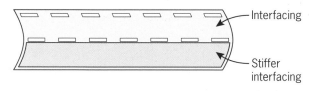

Interfacing

Stiffer interfacing

FIGURE 4 USE STIFFENED BANDING FOR A ROLL-RESISTANT WAISTBAND.

APPLYING WAISTBANDING

1 Fuse the banding to the wrong side of the fabric waistband.

2 Once cooled, fold the unnotched edge of the waistband to the wrong side, along the outer slotted line, and press.

3 Pin the other long edge to the waistline of the skirt or trousers, matching notches, and stitch it in place with a regular ⅝in (1.5cm) seam allowance. Note the stitching should fall within the slotted line. Trim the seam allowances and clip into the curves. Press the seam allowances towards the waistband.

4 Fold the waistband, right sides together, along the central slotted line and stitch the short ends. Trim the corners and turn the waistband back through.

5 Pin the neatened edge over the seam line on the wrong side of the waistband. Either slip stitch it in place or stitch in the ditch from the right side, catching the inside of the waistband in place as you stitch.

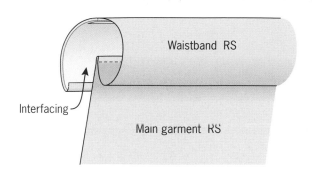

Waistband RS

Interfacing

Main garment RS

FIGURE 5 FOLD THE WAISTBAND OVER, WRONG SIDES TOGETHER, ALONG THE SLOTTED LINE, AFTER STITCHING THE SHORT ENDS. THE SHORT ENDS ARE SHOWN UNSTITCHED HERE FOR ILLUSTRATION PURPOSES ONLY.

HEMMING TAPES

Hemming tapes and hem webbing provide a very quick solution to hem finishing and ensure a completely invisible hem with no stitching involved.

Hem webbing is a double-sided fusible strip that looks like lightweight interfacing, but is simply a fused strip of adhesive.

1 Once the hem allowance is folded up and the raw edge neatened if necessary, lay the tape between the fabric layers of the hem, making sure the webbing is completely covered by the fabric.

2 Press the webbing in place with a hot iron, using a press cloth to protect the fabric. The heat melts the adhesive, sticking the fabric layers together.

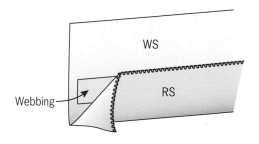

WS

RS

Webbing

FIGURE 6 PLACE THE HEM WEBBING BETWEEN THE FABRIC LAYERS AND BOND IT WITH A HOT IRON.

Hem tape is similar to hem webbing, but has a paper backing and is narrower, which makes it suitable for narrow hems.

1 Press the neatened hem allowance to the wrong side.

2 Open out the hem allowance and lay the tape on the hem allowance, paper side uppermost.

3 Press the tape in place and then remove the paper backing. Refold the hem and press it place.

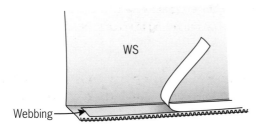

FIGURE 7 APPLY THE HEM TAPE TO THE HEM ALLOWANCE BEFORE REMOVING THE BACKING AND PRESSING THE HEM IN PLACE.

EXPERT TIP

To avoid unsightly ridges showing through on the right side of fabric, place the webbing or tape ¼in (6mm) from the neatened edge and press, without pressing the actual neatened edge.

SPECIALIST TAPES

There are other special tapes designed to help with garment construction and give support in specific areas. These include bias tape, edge tape and paper-backed fusible web.

Bias tape is a narrow fusible tape, cut on the bias so that it will bend around curves smoothly. It has a stitched line down the centre and should be applied to areas such as armholes and neck edges that need stabilizing and stitched down the centre to prevent unwanted stretch. Fuse the tape within the seam allowance, to the wrong side of the garment edge.

Edge tape is very similar to bias tape, but not cut on the bias. It is also fusible and used to prevent unwanted stretch and stabilize areas that require support, such as on shoulders, V-necklines, etc.

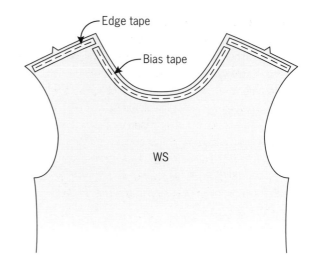

FIGURE 8 APPLY BIAS TAPE AROUND CURVED EDGES AND EDGE TAPE ALONG STRAIGHT ONES THAT NEED STABILIZING.

EXPERT TIP

To create a perfectly invisible blind hem, fuse a strip of edge tape to the back of the garment fabric within the hem allowance and hand stitch the hem, stitching only through the tape and the hem allowance.

Edgefix tape is similar to waistbanding but with the slotted line close to one edge. The tape can be fused along areas that are to be folded, with the slots along the fold line, in order to provide a crisp neat fold. This is ideal for self-faced edge-to-edge jackets or for creating crisp pleats or hems.

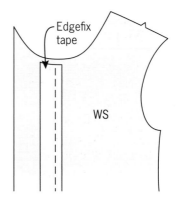

FIGURE 9 APPLY EDGEFIX TAPE SO THAT THE SLOTS LINE UP WITH THE FOLD LINE.

Paper-backed fusible web is a double-sided webbing with paper backing, available in sheets or by the metre. It is used to anchor appliqué and trims in position instead of, or before, stitching. Iron the fusible side onto the reverse of the appliqué fabric or trim. Once cooled, cut out the appliqué shape, peel off the paper backing and position the motif, adhesive side down, on the main fabric.

Stabilizer Similar to interfacing, stabilizer is used to provide a backing for densely stitched areas, thus reducing the risk of the fabric puckering. There is a huge range available, from traditional tearaway and fusible varieties to soluble or heat-away stabilizers, which disintegrate when ironed (after the stitching is complete). Choose the appropriate product to suit the fabric being stitched and whether the stabilizer will be encased or needs to disappear. For most applications, the stabilizer is applied to the back of the main fabric. However occasionally, for example to support dense stitching on pile fabrics, a soluble layer of stabilizer should also be used on the right side of the fabric to prevent the decorative stitches sinking into the pile.

EXPERT TIP

If embroidering on lightweight fabrics, sandwich the fabric between two layers of soluble stabilizer, which can be washed away once the stitching is complete. This will help prevent the fabric being pulled into the feed dogs and/or puckering under the weight of the stitching. Also use a soluble stabilizer behind button-holes on lightweight chiffons or voiles. Once stitched the stabilizer can be washed away to leave delicate but perfectly formed buttonholes.

UNDERLINING

An underlining is an additional layer of fabric used to stabilize loosely woven fabrics, strengthen lightweight delicate fabrics or eliminate transparency where it is not wanted.

Underlining differs from lining and, indeed, both can be used in the same garment. Underlining is usually made from cotton broadcloth or silk organza, but can be any suitable material that works with the main fabric and has the same laundering requirements. A lining is used to give the garment body, help it to hang smoothly, conceal seams and, when made from a slippery fabric, help the garment to slip on and off easily.

Underlining will alter the handle of the fashion fabric because it adds weight and bulk. The extent to which it alters the main fabric will depend on the material used. Soft cotton batiste or cotton broadcloth works well for wools, wool crepe, etc. while a silk organza to underline silk will minimize the change. Another way to minimize altering the fluidity of the main fabric is to underline the lining instead.

APPLYING UNDERLINING

1 Use the same pattern pieces for the underlining as for the main garment sections excluding the collar, cuffs, facings and waistband.

2 Transfer any pattern markings from the tissue to the right side of the underlining sections. Then pin them to the main fabric pieces, wrong sides together.

3 Hand baste the underlining to the main fabric through the centre of the darts, down through the foldline and around the edges, basting approximately ½in (1.3cm) from the edge.

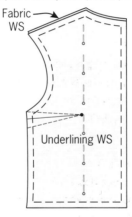

Fabric WS

Underlining WS

FIGURE 10 BASTE THE UNDERLINING PIECES TO THE MAIN FABRIC.

4 Now treat the underlining and the main fabric as one layer and construct the garment according to the pattern instructions.

STYLISH SKIRTS

A SELECTION OF SKIRTS CAN EXTEND YOUR MIX-AND-MATCH OUTFIT OPTIONS ENORMOUSLY. A SIMPLE SKIRT IS ALSO ONE OF THE EASIEST GARMENTS TO MAKE, YET CAN LOOK A MILLION DOLLARS IF MADE WELL IN A GOOD QUALITY FABRIC. DRESS UP A SKIRT WITH A JACKET, MAKE IT IN A GLAMOROUS FABRIC FOR EVENING OR TEAM IT WITH A CASUAL TOP FOR EVERYDAY WEAR.

SKIRTS CAN BE ANY LENGTH, FITTED AND SLIM, ELASTICATED FOR COMFORT, A-LINE OR HAVE SWING AND FULLNESS ADDED WITH EXTRA FABRIC PANELS. THEY REQUIRE CASINGS, FACINGS, WAISTBANDS OR CLOSURES SUCH AS ZIPPERS, BUTTONS AND BUTTONHOLES, HOOKS AND EYES — ALL COVERED IN THIS CHAPTER.

TOP 10 SKIRT STYLES

ADAPT ANY OF THESE TOP TEN SHAPES TO CREATE A WARDROBE OF SKIRT SHAPES TO SUIT EVERY OCCASION.

STRAIGHT SKIRT

This elegant and slim-fitting style will suit every figure when worn to the correct length. Although slim Jims can wear any length, apple- or pear-shaped figures look best in knee length. To elongate the silhouette, petite figures can match hosiery colour to the skirt. Straight skirts may have front and back darts at the waist to ensure a close fit and often have a side or centre back slit to give a wider hem. A pencil skirt is similar, with narrowed shaping below the hip for an even slimmer fit.

Fabrics: Gabardine, flannel, lightweight woollens, duchess satin, crepe and crepe-back satin, medium-weight cotton mix (preferably with Lycra®), denim

Special techniques: Making darts and facings, inserting zipper and waistbanding
Ease of sewing: Easy–intermediate

A-LINE SKIRT

On an A-line skirt the side seams are at an angle to give the shaping. It is a good style to balance the bust and hips. It will also show off a bold fabric print well as there is minimal seaming, the design usually comprising of one front piece and two back pieces with a centre back zipper. An even simpler version has a single front and back, with a side zip. Hem lines can be straight, asymmetrical or shaped.

Fabrics: Cottons, gabardine, satins, linens and linen look, crepe, raw silk, silk dupion

Special techniques: Inserting zipper and waistbanding, sewing bias-cut seams, making facings
Ease of sewing: Easy–intermediate

PANELLED SKIRT

This style adds fullness and flare with shaped panels that fit smoothly from waist to hip and then flare out to the hem. They can be made with four, six or eight panels and have a side or centre back zipper. The more flared the panels, the greater the hem width. This is an easy design to fit as you can make small adjustments in the multi-seaming.

Fabrics: Challis, silks, cottons, velvet, medium-weight woollens, gabardine, lightweight denim

Special techniques: Inserting zippers, making facing or waistband, sewing bias seams

Ease of sewing: Easy–intermediate

SKIRT WITH GODETS

Another method of creating fullness, godets are fabric inserts added to the bottom third of the skirt. The top part of the skirt can be fitted with darts, panels or even have an elasticated waist. Godets can be triangular or shaped but are always wider at the bottom edge. The more godets added, the wider the hem will be. Variations include a straight skirt, with a deep ruffled section added below the hip.

Fabrics: Lightweight floaty fabrics such as georgette, silks, lightweight cottons, satin, viscose or silk velvet

Special techniques: Accurate pivoting for corners and curves on the seaming, inserting zipper

Ease of sewing: Intermediate

PLEATED SKIRT

Regular folds in the fabric add volume and flare to increase the width and give a full A-line shaped skirt. Pleats can be knife-edge, inverted or box (see Chapter 7). To avoid too much bulk over the tummy and hips, pleats can be stitched down for the first 4–6in (10–15cm). This is a good design for slim figures, but best avoided if pear-shaped.

Fabrics: Lightweight woollens, gabardine, medium-weight silks such as raw silk and silk dupion, linen-look

Special techniques: Making pleats, inserting zippers

Ease of sewing: Intermediate

YOKED SKIRT

This skirt style has a shaped band, wider than a waistband, that fits smoothly from the waist to high hip. The skirt below can then be pleated, gathered or straight A-line. This is a good design if you like the fullness of pleats, but wish to have a slimmer silhouette over the waist and tummy.

Fabrics: Medium-weight silks, polyesters or cottons, crepe, crepe-back satin, gabardine

Special techniques: Inserting zipper and waistbanding, joining disproportionate seams

Ease of sewing: Intermediate

WRAP SKIRT

Generally a casual style and great for holiday wear, wrap skirts are quick to make, with minimal fitting. Closure is usually made with side ties or a single button on a faced waist or waistband. A mock wrap has a front panel attached at the waistband and is more suitable for general wear.

Fabrics: Cottons, batiks, silks for wrap; gabardine, flannel, lightweight wool for mock wrap

Special techniques: Making ties or buttonholes, top stitching

Ease of sewing: Easy

TIERED SKIRT

Made from panels of increasing width and length, this is a casual, free-falling soft skirt style ideal for lightweight summery fabrics. Called peasant or gypsy skirts, the horizontal panels can be the same or coordinating fabrics. The waist can be faced, have a waistband or be elasticated for an easy, comfortable fit.

Fabrics: Lightweight cottons, georgette, cheesecloth, seersucker

Special techniques: Gathering, making elastic casing, inserting waistbanding

Ease of sewing: Easy

BUBBLE SKIRT

Also known as a puff-ball, this design comes and goes in and out of fashion. It has an inner lining, shorter and straighter than the outer fabric, which is then sewn to the lining at the hem to allow the main fabric to balloon out. It is usually made for party wear or special occasions.

Fabrics: Those with some body to create the bubble, such as cottons, medium-weight raw silk, silk dupion, satin

Special techniques: Joining disproportional seams, gathering, inserting zipper

Ease of sewing: Intermediate

BIAS-CUT SKIRT

The fabric is cut on the bias for this style, which produces a soft, floaty silhouette. It can flatter most figure types as the fabric skims the body, clinging where it touches. Mostly used for special occasion wear, evening wear and summer skirts, this style is often made from two layers, an under skirt in silk or satin with over skirt in transparent chiffon. A faced or elasticated waist adds to the simplicity.

Fabrics: Floaty, lightweight fabrics such as georgette, silks, lightweight satin, chiffon, polyester, viscose

Special techniques Cutting on the bias, sewing bias seams

Easy of sewing: Easy

CASINGS, FACINGS AND WAISTBANDS

SKIRTS, TROUSERS AND SHORTS CAN BE
FINISHED AT THE WAIST WITH A CHOICE OF
WAISTBAND, FACING OR CASING FOR ELASTIC
(AS WELL AS WITH A BINDING OR A YOKE).
THE BEST CHOICE DEPENDS ON THE STYLE
OF THE GARMENT AND WHETHER IT IS SMART,
CASUAL OR COMFORT FIT.

CASINGS

The simplest finish for a waistline is a casing for elastic or a drawstring, which makes an easy wear, easy fit garment. The casing is simply a tunnel through which the cord or elastic is fed. It can be made by turning the top of the garment down and stitching it in place, or by attaching an additional strip of fabric. Casings are also used to elasticate the waistlines of trousers and easy fit dresses. Elastic of 1in (2.5cm) width gives a more flattering line than narrow ¼in (6mm) elastic.

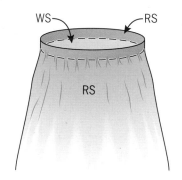

FIGURE 1 USE A CASING TO MAKE AN EXPANDING WAISTLINE.

Stylish skirt

Our stylish skirt is made in a soft viscose velvet. It has an elasticated waist, finished with the all-in-one casing method (see p. 65), and an added flounce at the hem line.

❀ **The pattern is Simplicity 3894.**

MAKING A SELF-CASING

1 When cutting out the fabric, extend the height of the garment on the waistline by the width of the elastic, plus ½in (1.3cm) for turnings and allowances. A commercial pattern with an elasticated waist will already incorporate the casing allowance.

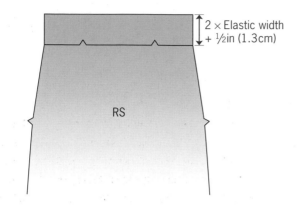

2 × Elastic width + ½in (1.3cm)

RS

FIGURE 2 MAKE SURE YOU ADD SUFFICIENT EXTRA FABRIC TO MAKE THE CASING.

2 After any side seams have been stitched and pressed, fold half the casing allowance to the inside of the garment and press. Then fold the raw edge under by ¼in (6mm) and press again.

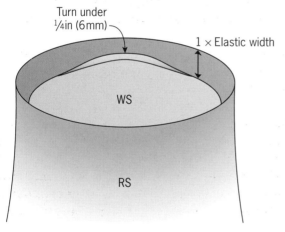

Turn under ¼in (6mm)

1 × Elastic width

WS

RS

FIGURE 3 FOLD THE ALLOWANCE OVER TO MAKE THE CASING.

EXPERT TIP

Before stitching the casing, and to avoid problems later with feeding the elastic through it, anchor the garment seam allowances by fusing them in place with a little hemming web.

3 Stitch the casing to the garment along the lower fold, leaving an opening of approximately 1½in (4cm) for inserting the elastic later.

4 Stitch all around the casing again a scant ⅛in (3mm) from the

top fold. Make sure the space between the rows of stitching is slightly wider than the elastic width.

5 Measure the length of elastic required; that is the waist measurement less 1in (2.5cm). Pin one end of the elastic just outside the casing and, slipping a safety pin through the other end, feed it through the casing all the way around and out again. Overlap the ends of elastic and machine stitch them together securely.

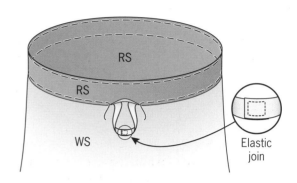

RS

RS

WS

Elastic join

FIGURE 4 THREAD THE ELASTIC THROUGH THE CASING AND NEATLY SECURE THE ENDS.

SEWING SENSE

Before stitching the elastic ends together, safety pin them in place and try the garment on to check for fit and comfort. Adjust if necessary and then stitch the ends together.

6 To prevent the elastic twisting inside the casing, stitch vertically from the top of the casing to the bottom through all thicknesses at the side seams.

EXPERT TIP

To create a frill above the casing, add an extra 1–2in (2.5–5cm) to the casing allowance. When the casing has been folded and the lower edge stitched in place, mark the top stitching line the elastic width, plus ⅛in (3mm) for ease, up from the lower line. Then stitch along the marked line, leaving a frill above the casing.

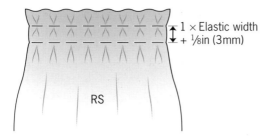

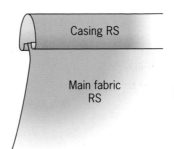

↕ 1 × Elastic width
+ ⅛in (3mm)

RS

FIGURE 5 STITCH THE CASING WITH JUST ENOUGH SPACE FOR THE ELASTIC, LEAVING THE FRILL ABOVE.

ATTACHING CASING

This is an alternative casing technique, which can be used on dress waists, on contoured waists that have shaping or on heavyweight fabrics where a self-casing would be too thick. An attached casing can be made from contrast fabric or bias binding.

1 Cut the casing fabric on the bias, twice the elastic width plus 1½in (3.5cm) for turnings and allowances, and as long as the circumference of the garment. Alternatively, you could use bias binding.

2 Machine stitch the right side of one long edge of the casing to the right side of the top edge of the garment, taking a regular ⅝in (1.5cm) seam. Press the seam allowances towards the casing.

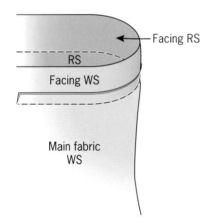

— Facing RS

RS

Facing WS

Main fabric
WS

FIGURE 6 ATTACH THE CASING AND PRESS THE SEAM ALLOWANCES TOWARDS IT.

3 Fold the other long edge of the casing to the wrong side by ⅝in (1.5cm) and press. Fold the casing in half and pin the neatened long edge over the seam. Working from the right side, machine stitch the casing edge in place, leaving an opening for feeding elastic through. Continue with steps 5 and 6 on p. 64 as for a self-casing.

Casing RS

Main fabric
RS

FIGURE 7 FOLD THE CASING OVER TO THE WRONG SIDE OF THE MAIN FABRIC AND STITCH THE EDGE IN PLACE.

EXPERT TIP

To create an applied casing for the inside of a dress, cut a length of bias binding the circumference of the ungathered dress plus ½in (1.3cm) for overlap. Press the two short ends under. Then stitch the casing in place on the dress along both long edges, making sure the rows of stitches are far enough apart for the elastic. Feed the elastic through the overlap, secure it and then slip stitch the opening closed.

MAKING ALL-IN-ONE CASING

An alternative method of creating an elastic waist is to attach the elastic directly to the top edge of the garment and then turn the fabric down to create a casing with the elastic attached. This method is often used on sportswear and knitted garments.

1 Determine the length of elastic required; that is the waist measurement less 1in (2.5cm). Then overlap and stitch the ends together to create a continuous circle of elastic.

2 Divide the elastic into quarters. Also divide the top edge of the garment into quarters, ideally on the side seams, centre front and centre back. On the wrong side of the garment, pin the join in the elastic to the centre back of the garment, then the quarter marks to the side seams and centre front, matching the pinned quarters and with the edge of the elastic on the top edge of the fabric.

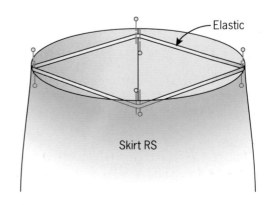

— Elastic

Skirt RS

FIGURE 8 PIN THE ELASTIC TO THE GARMENT AT EQUAL INTERVALS.

3 Zigzag stitch or overlock (with the knife disengaged) the elastic to the top edge of the garment, stretching it between the pins to fit.

4 Fold the top edge of the garment to the inside, encasing the elastic. To hold it in place, either pin or stitch vertically down through all thicknesses at the side seams, centre front and centre back. Then stitch again, close to the lower edge of the casing, stretching the elastic to fit.

FACINGS

Facings provide a neat finish to the neck, waist and armholes without the need for collars, waistbands or sleeves. They are usually cut from the same fabric as the main garment, but where this is bulky or highly textured are better cut from lining fabric, which will reduce bulk and possible skin irritation.

Most facings are made from separate pattern pieces. The exception is a self-faced jacket front, which is formed from an extended jacket section that folds back on itself to form the facing.

APPLYING FACINGS

Commercial patterns provide separate pattern pieces for the facings. However, if making your own to replace a collar or waistband, start with the pattern piece for the garment section to be faced.

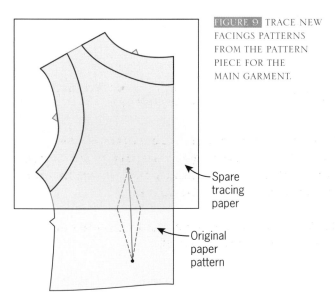

FIGURE 9 TRACE NEW FACINGS PATTERNS FROM THE PATTERN PIECE FOR THE MAIN GARMENT.

— Spare tracing paper

— Original paper pattern

1 Lay a spare piece of tissue paper over the pattern and trace along the top edge, matching the notches. Trace along the side edges for approximately 3in (7.5cm). Then draw in the bottom edge of the facing, following the curve of the top edge.

2 Cut out the facing in fabric and interfacing. Apply the interfacing to the wrong side of the facings (see p. 56).

3 If applicable, join the front facings to the back facings and press the seams open. Neaten the outer edges of the facing with overlock stitch or by turning under the seam allowance, clipping and notching around the curves so it will lay flat, and then top stitching it in place.

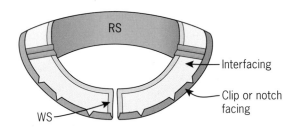

FIGURE 10 PIECE THE FACING TOGETHER AND NEATEN THE OUTER EDGES.

4 Prevent unwanted stretch by stay stitching the garment edges with regular stitch length just inside seam line.

5 With right sides together, machine stitch the facings to the garment, matching the side seams, centre back/front, etc.and taking a ⅝in (1.5cm) seam allowance. Trim the seam allowances, clipping and notching around the curves (see p. 26). On medium- to heavyweight fabrics, grade the seam allowances (see p. 26) to reduce bulk in the seams.

6 Press the seam allowances towards the facing. Open out the facing so that it is to the right of the garment. Then understitch (see p. 25) on the facing close to the previous seaming and stitching through the seam allowance underneath.

7 Fold the facing to the wrong side of the garment, rolling the seam so it sits just inside. If desired, edge stitch the facing in place, using matching thread and stitching a scant ⅛in (3mm) from the garment edge.

WAISTBANDS

A waistband may be wide or narrow, shaped or straight, with an overlapped end at the side, front or back opening. To ensure a comfortable fit, the finished waistband should be ⅜–1in (1–2.5cm) larger than the waist size.

Commercial patterns provide pattern pieces for any waistbanding needed. However, if you want to add your own, determine the length of the waistband needed by measuring the waist and then adding the following measurements:

- 1in (2.5cm) for wearing ease
- 1¼in (3cm) for seam allowances (⅝in (1.5cm) at each end)
- 1¼in (3cm) of buttonhole/closure overlap

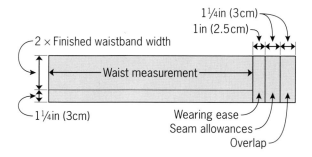

FIGURE 11 ADD EXTRA ALLOWANCES TO THE BASIC WAIST AND WAISTBAND MEASUREMENTS.

The width of waistband is down to personal choice, ranging from a narrow band of ⅝in (1.5cm) to a wide 2in (5cm). To calculate the amount of fabric needed, double the finished width and add 1¼in (3cm) for seam allowances.

EXPERT TIP

A straight, wider band can look very effective but will sit higher above the waist and may crease and roll. So, if a wide band is desired, shape it on the lower edge to fit around the upper hips and then lower the top edge of the garment by a corresponding amount. The top of the waistband will then sit at the waist.

APPLYING WAISTBANDS

1 Cut fabric and interfacing for the waistband to size, as calculated above. Apply the interfacing to the wrong side of the fabric (or use waistbanding interfacing, see p. 57).

2 Stitch the waistband sections together if necessary. Then neaten one long edge by overlocking or turning under ⅝in (1.5cm) and top stitching it in place.

3 With right sides together, stitch the unneatened long edge of the waistband to the garment waistline, with one short end overlapping the garment opening by ⅝in (1.5cm) and the other by 1⅞in (4.5cm).

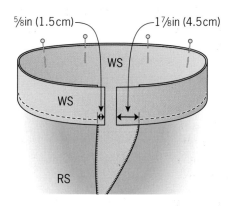

FIGURE 12 STITCH ONE LONG EDGE OF THE WAISTBAND TO THE GARMENT.

4 Grade the seam allowances and press the seams towards the waistband.

5 Fold the waistband in half, right sides together, so that the neatened edge will sit just over the seam line. Stitch across the shorter end. On the overlapping end, stitch down from the fold, pivot and stitch along to the garment edge so that the stitching is in line with the seam attaching the waistband to the garment.

6 Trim the seam allowances, cutting the corners at an angle and clipping into the corner where the waistband meets the garment.

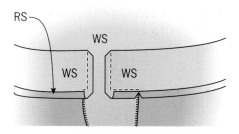

FIGURE 14 STITCH THE ENDS OF THE WAISTBAND AND THEN TRIM AND CLIP INTO THE SEAM ALLOWANCES.

7 Turn the waistband through, using a point turner for the corners. Pin the neatened edge over the seam line and either slip stitch it in place or machine stitch-in-the-ditch (see p. 25) from the front, catching the waistbanding in place.

8 Finish the waistband with a button and buttonhole or with hooks and eyes (see pp. 73 and 75).

CLOSURES

GARMENTS NEED SOME SORT OF OPENING TO GET THEM OVER THE HEAD, BUST OR HIPS, SO THERE ARE VARIOUS CLOSURE METHODS TO CONSIDER. PRIMARILY THESE INCLUDE ZIPPERS, BUTTONS AND BUTTONHOLES, OR HOOKS AND EYES. THESE ARE OFTEN THE ELEMENTS OF DRESSMAKING THAT PUT NEWCOMERS OFF, BUT WITH A FEW SIMPLE STEPS, ALL ARE EASILY ACHIEVABLE.

ZIPPERS

Without wishing to complicate the matter, there are different types of zipper (as well as various ways of inserting them), including:

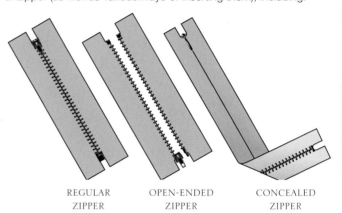

| REGULAR ZIPPER | OPEN-ENDED ZIPPER | CONCEALED ZIPPER |

Regular zippers are fixed closed at one end and come in a wide range of colours and lengths, including continuous zipper on the roll so you can buy the exact length you require. Choices include cotton tape with metal zipper teeth for jeans, trousers and other garments that require a sturdy fastening; lighter weight nylon zipper tape with moulded teeth for dresses, skirts, etc.; and decorative zippers with clear, crystal, silver-coated or coloured teeth.

Open-ended zippers can be completely unfastened and so are suitable for jackets and coats. They can also have metal or plastic teeth and come in different weights for different applications. Double-ended zippers have two zipper pulls so they can be opened at both ends. These zippers can be inserted using either the lapped or centred method.

Invisible/concealed zippers have the teeth coiled on the underside and, when inserted, all that is visible from the right side of the garment is the tiny zipper pull. No stitching is visible from the right side of the garment. Invisible zippers are used in skirts, dresses and bodices.

Straight Skirt

This classic straight skirt is made in dress-weight denim, combining a traditional style with fashion fabric. It has a comfortable contoured yoke at the waist and a back zipper. Bias binding and a ribbon trim have also been applied around the mock pocket flaps.

❀ **The pattern is Simplicity 2475.**

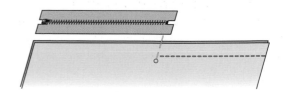

EXPERT TIP

If the correct length of zipper is not available, choose a longer one. Then mark the required length on the zipper tape and bar stitch (stitch on the spot) across the teeth at the required length to create a new zipper stop. Leaving a ⅝in (1.5cm) seam allowance, cut off the excess.

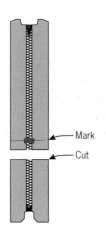

FIGURE 1 SHORTEN A LONGER ZIPPER BY BAR STITCHING ACROSS IT AT THE REQUIRED LENGTH AND TRIMMING THE EXCESS.

Mark

Cut

INSERTING A LAPPED ZIPPER

Used on skirts, in the side seam on trousers and on the back seams of dresses, a lapped zipper has only one flap of fabric that laps over the zipper. Thus only one row of stitching is visible.

1 Separately neaten each of the seam allowances of the seam that the zipper is to be inserted into. Pin the seam together and then lay the zipper in position, leaving space for the seam, waistband or facing at the top of the garment. Mark the bottom of the zipper on the seam.

2 Remove the zipper and then machine stitch from the marked position to the end of the seam, reverse stitching at the marked point to secure the thread ends. Press the seam allowances open.

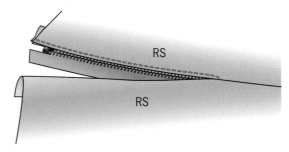

FIGURE 2 MARK THE LENGTH OF THE ZIPPER AND MACHINE STITCH THE REST OF THE SEAM.

3 Working on a flat surface, place the zipper right side up and the zipper opening on the garment wrong side down over the zipper. Pin the right-hand, folded seam allowance to the zipper tape and then machine stitch it in place close to the fold and the teeth.

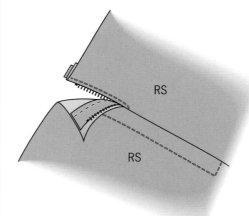

RS

RS

FIGURE 3 STITCH THE SEAM ALLOWANCE TO THE ZIPPER, CLOSE TO THE FOLD AND TEETH.

4 With the right side of the garment still uppermost, check that the zipper is smooth and flat. Then baste the left-hand side of the zipper to the garment through all thicknesses, including the zipper tape, and approximately ½in (1.3cm) from the seam line. Starting from the seam line at the bottom of the zipper, machine stitch about ½in (1.3cm). Then pivot and stitch up the side of the zipper following the basting stitches.

RS

RS

FIGURE 4 BASTE AND THEN MACHINE STITCH THE SECOND SIDE OF THE ZIPPER IN PLACE.

SEWING SENSE
Stitch from the bottom of the zipper to prevent wrinkles appearing at the base.

INSERTING A CENTRED ZIPPER

Used on dresses with centre back seams and on zipped jackets and coats, a centred zipper is inserted to give two equal flaps that meet in the middle, usually concealing the zipper teeth below.

1 Follow step 1 on p. 71 for lapped zippers. Then hand or machine baste the seam from the top to the marked point. Change to the regular stitch length and machine stitch from the marked position to the end of the seam, reversing at the marked point to secure the stitching.

2 With the garment wrong side up, pin the zipper in place, right side down over the pressed open seam allowances so that the zipper teeth are centred over the seam. Pin and baste all around the zipper through all the thicknesses.

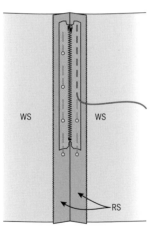

FIGURE 5 PIN AND THEN BASTE THE ZIPPER IN POSITION CENTRALLY OVER THE SEAM ALLOWANCES.

WS   WS

RS

3 Turn the work to the right side and, with the zipper foot attached, machine stitch a few stitches from the seam line at the base of the zipper. Then pivot and stitch up the side of the zipper, following the basting line. Repeat for the other side of the zipper, again starting at the base.

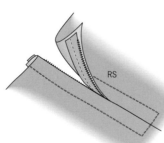

RS

FIGURE 6 STITCH ALONG EACH SIDE OF THE ZIPPER SEAM, EACH TIME STARTING AT THE BASE OF THE ZIPPER.

SEWING SENSE

To sew smoothly past the zipper pull, stop with the needle down about 1in (2.5cm) from the pull, raise the presser foot and then gently ease the zipper pull down below the needle. Lower the presser foot and continue stitching.

INSERTING AN INVISIBLE ZIPPER

An invisible zipper is inserted in a similar method to a centred one, but before the rest of the seam is stitched. To sew it in place invisibly, it is best to use a special invisible zipper foot, which has deep grooves on the underside through which the zipper teeth are guided. Using this method means that it is not possible to stitch to the very end of the zipper, so buy one at least 1in (2.5cm) longer than the pattern suggests.

Top

Underside

INVISIBLE ZIPPER FOOT

1 Press the seam allowances to the wrong side to create a crease at the seam line. Open the seam allowances out.

EXPERT TIP

Open the zipper and press the coils of the teeth open so you can stitch closer to the teeth.

2 With the left-hand garment section right side up, place the opened zipper, right side down on the garment, so that the teeth are uppermost and line up with the seam line crease. Baste the zipper in place down the centre of the tape.

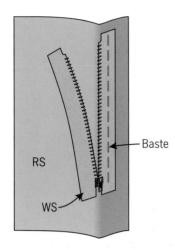

FIGURE 7 BASTE THE CENTRE OF THE LEFT-HAND ZIPPER TAPE TO THE LEFT-HAND GARMENT SECTION.

Baste

RS

WS

3 Using an invisible zipper foot, stitch the tape in place only on the seam allowance, stitching very close to the zipper teeth and as far down the tape as possible. As you stitch, the coils of the teeth are guided through the groove of the foot, slightly opening so that the stitching is formed virtually under the teeth. Secure the stitching.

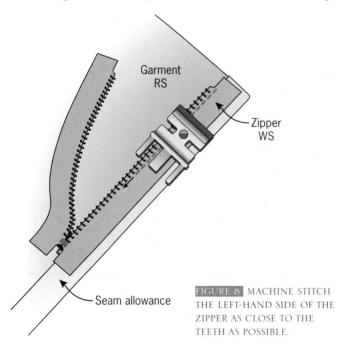

Garment RS

Zipper WS

Seam allowance

FIGURE 8 MACHINE STITCH THE LEFT-HAND SIDE OF THE ZIPPER AS CLOSE TO THE TEETH AS POSSIBLE.

4 Close the zipper and position the right-hand side of the garment over the left side with the seam allowances even. Pin the zipper in place to the right-hand seam allowance, again aligning the teeth along the crease of the seam line. Open the zipper and stitch it in place as in step 3 on p. 71, but with the teeth feeding through the other groove of the presser foot.

5 Pin the rest of the seam together. Change to a regular zipper presser foot and stitch from the base of the zipper to the end of the seam, securing the stitching at each end.

SEWING SENSE

To prevent the zipper tape flapping about at the base, stitch it to the seam allowances.

BUTTONHOLES

A buttonhole usually comprises three or four bar tacks at each end of two parallel rows of satin stitch. Making buttonholes used to be tricky, but with modern sewing machines, they are a breeze! Many machines have a one-step buttonhole function, others take three or more steps, but each section is automatically sewn. Here are some general tips for making successful buttonholes (see also bound buttonholes on p. 130).

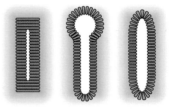

THREE TYPES OF BUTTONHOLE

SEWING SENSE

Always test stitch buttonholes, with the same number of fabric layers and interfacing, before working on a garment.

Backing One key requirement to successful buttonholes is to back the area with a suitable interfacing or stabilizer to provide support for the concentrated stitching, as well as help the buttonhole retain its shape during use. With interfacing or stabilizer in place, buttonholes can be stitched even on chiffon or thick woollen coating. On waistbands, facings, collars and cuffs, the interfacing will already be in place. Buttonholes on a blouse or shirt front may need a backing added. For very fine, lightweight fabric, this can be tearaway or soluble stabilizer, which can be removed once the buttonhole is stitched, or for transparent fabrics you can use an extra layer or two of the fashion fabric.

Thread Most buttonholes can be stitched with general-purpose sewing thread. However, if making small buttonholes on delicate silks, satins, etc., use silk thread. For heavyweight coatings, use a buttonhole thread, which is stronger and thicker.

Needles Use a new sharp needle for woven fabrics or a ballpoint needle for knit fabrics so that it can easily penetrate the layers of fabric and interfacing.

Buttonhole size Many modern machines have a nifty buttonhole foot into which you place the button so that the hole fits the button perfectly. However, if your machine doesn't have this, determine the buttonhole size by measuring the diameter of a flat button and adding ⅛in (3mm) wriggle room. For a domed button or one with a shank, measure around the button, halve the measurement and add ⅛in (3mm).

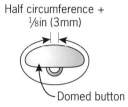

Diameter +
⅛in (3mm)

Half circumference +
⅛in (3mm)

Flat button

Domed button

FIGURE 9 MEASURE THE BUTTON AND ADD EXTRA FOR EASE.

POSITIONING BUTTONHOLES

Buttonholes should be positioned at least ¾in (2cm) from the garment edge. As a general rule, they are positioned 2–3in (5–8cm) apart. Site them closer together on lightweight fabrics.

For blouses and shirts, stitch horizontal buttonholes in a row, evenly spaced. Start with one at the fullest bust point and then space the rest evenly above and below. If working without a paper pattern (which will have buttonhole positions marked), draw two vertical lines the buttonhole width apart. Then mark the buttonhole positions evenly spaced like the rungs of a ladder.

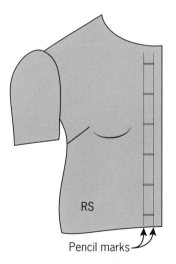

RS

Pencil marks

FIGURE 10 MARK HORIZONTAL BUTTONHOLES. EVENLY SPACED.

For vertical buttonholes, mark one chalk line ¾in (2cm) from the garment edge. Then mark the buttonholes, evenly spaced down the line. Mark the top of the buttonhole in one colour and the bottom in a different colour so you can easily see which mark is the beginning of a buttonhole and which a space.

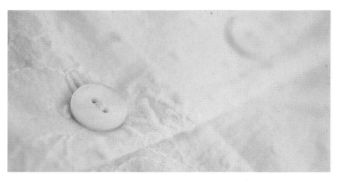

OPENING A BUTTONHOLE

The easiest way to cut open a buttonhole is to use a seam ripper. Place a pin just inside the bar tacks at one end of the buttonhole and, from the other end, push the blade between the two rows of satin stitch towards the pin.

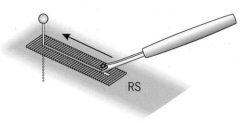

RS

FIGURE 11 PUSH THE BLADE BETWEEN THE ROWS OF STITCHES TOWARDS THE PIN.

MAKING A CORDED BUTTONHOLE

To make a stronger buttonhole for jackets, coats, etc., encase a length of cord within the buttonhole stitching. This can be anything from thin string to crochet thread as it will be completely covered.

1 Wrap the cord around the hook at the back of the buttonhole foot, holding the two ends in front of the foot. As you stitch the two parallel rows, the satin stitch will go over the cord.

2 Once finished, feed the ends of cord through to the reverse of the fabric or trim them very close to the buttonhole stitching.

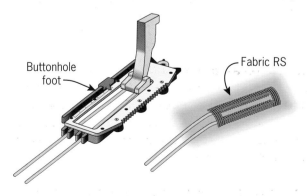

Buttonhole foot

Fabric RS

FIGURE 12 LOOP THE CORD AROUND THE HOOK ON THE BUTTONHOLE FOOT AND STITCH OVER IT TO GIVE A STRONG BUTTONHOLE WITH SLIGHTLY RAISED STITCHING.

MAKING BUTTON LOOPS

An alternative to buttonholes and often used on bridal or special occasion wear, button loops are also a good choice on very thick fabrics where a buttonhole is difficult to sew or for unusually shaped buttons. The loops can be made from any woven fabric or braid to complement the garment. Ready-made loops are also available for bridal and special occasion wear.

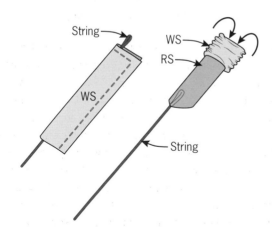

1 Cut a bias strip of fabric the length needed by ¾in (2cm) wide. Also cut a length of string 5in (1.3cm) longer.

2 Fold the bias fabric, right sides together, along the length, sandwiching the string in the fold. Stitch across one short end, catching the string, and then stitch down the long edge.

FIGURE 13 STITCH THE STRING INTO THE FABRIC AND THEN PULL ON IT TO TURN THE LOOPS THROUGH.

3 Leaving the seam allowance intact and pulling on the string, turn the fabric through. Cut off the string and set it aside to use again.

4 Measure the button diameter. Then divide the loop fabric into equal lengths to go round the buttons, adding a total of 1¼in (3cm) to each length for seam allowances.

5 With the garment right side up, pin the loops in place, so that the raw ends of the loops are in line with the raw edge of the fabric. Baste the loops in position.

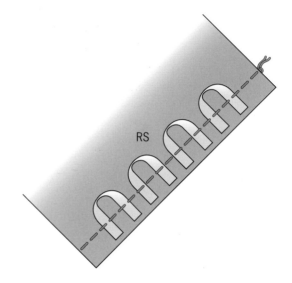

FIGURE 14 PIN AND THEN BASTE THE LOOPS IN POSITION ON THE MAIN FABRIC.

6 Position the facing and main fabric, right sides together, sandwiching the loops. Stitch the seam and then turn the facing to the underside so that the loops stand proud of the fabric.

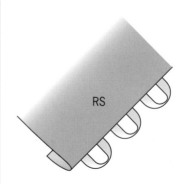

FIGURE 15 TURN THE FACING UNDER SO THAT THE LOOPS SIT ALONG THE EDGE OF THE GARMENT.

BUTTONS

Available shanked or to sew through, buttons come in all shapes, sizes and designs. Shanked buttons have a raised section underneath with a hole through which you stitch to attach it to a garment. They are better for medium- to heavyweight fabric where the button sits proud of the cloth, providing room for the buttoned layer. Sew-through buttons are flat and suitable for lightweight fabrics.

POSITIONING BUTTONS

To decide on the button positioning, overlap the buttonhole and place a pin approximately ⅛in (3mm) from the end nearest the garment edge on horizontal buttonholes or ⅛in (3mm) from the top of vertical buttonholes.

Available in plastic or metal, self-cover buttons offer an alternative option. Use a double layer of fabric or line the fabric with lightweight interfacing to prevent the button base showing through. Avoid very bulky fabrics or those that fray easily. Instead use a medium-weight fabric that complements the garment.

DIFFERENT TYPES OF BUTTONS

ATTACHING BUTTONS

Carefully remove the buttonhole fabric and then sew the button at the pin position, using a double length of thread. For buttonholes on coats and jackets, use buttonhole thread, which is thicker and much stronger.

If sewing a sew-through button onto heavier weight fabric, add a thread shank.

1 Place a toothpick or matchstick on top of the button and take three to six stitches over it.

2 Remove the stick, pull the button away from the fabric and wrap the thread around the loose stitches below the button to create a shank. Take the thread to the back of the work and tie off the ends to secure.

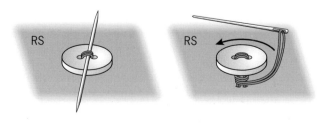

FIGURE 16 SEW THE BUTTON ON OVER A TOOTHPICK OR MATCHSTICK AND THEN WIND THREAD AROUND THE THREAD SHANK.

ALTERNATIVE FASTENERS

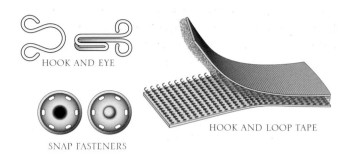

HOOK AND EYE

SNAP FASTENERS

HOOK AND LOOP TAPE

FIGURE 17 A HOOK AND EYE, PAIR OF SNAP FASTENERS AND A STRIP OF HOOK AND LOOP TAPE.

Hooks and eyes These are often used at the top of a zipper or instead of a button on a skirt waistband. Comprising of two parts, one a hook, the other a looped eye, different sizes are available to suit different types of garment, ranging from lightweight to heavy-duty varieties that can be used as fasteners on jackets and coats. Stitch the hook and eye in place using buttonhole thread or a double strand of regular thread that matches the garment.

Snap fasteners Also known as poppas, these are ideal for children's garments. They are made in clear plastic or metal, and available in packs or singly. They also come in different sizes and have two parts – one with a socket, the other with a raised ball that snaps snugly into the socket. Stitch the socket part on the overlap of the garment and the raised ball section on the underlap, so that the ball is facing away from the body. Ready-made snap tape is also available and particularly suited to baby clothes or bed linen. Separate the two halves and then stitch both long edges on each tape to two edges of the garment that need closing. Use a zipper foot to stitch as close as possible to the raised poppas.

Hook and loop tape Another two-part fastener, one tape has rows of tiny hooks and the other has a soft felt looped side into which the hooks sink and catch when the two pieces are pressed together. Stitch all around the edges of both tapes to attach. Position the loop side to the overlap of the garment and the hook side to the underlap, so that the abrasive side is facing away from the body.

DRESS FOR BEST

A DRESS IS A WONDERFUL ADDITION TO A CAPSULE WARDROBE. IT CAN BE CASUAL, COMFORTABLE, SMART, CHIC OR GLAMOROUS DEPENDING ON THE STYLE AND FABRIC USED. TEAM A DRESS WITH A BOLERO FOR EVENING WEAR, A SMART JACKET FOR THE OFFICE OR A CARDIGAN FOR CASUAL WEAR. MAKE IT MINI TO WEAR WITH LEGGINGS OR JEANS OR MAKE IT MAXI FOR SUNNY DAYS AND ELEGANT EVENINGS.

DRESSES REQUIRE SHAPING TO MOULD THE FABRIC AROUND THE BODY. THIS CHAPTER WILL SHOW YOU HOW TO MAKE DARTS, PLEATS, TUCKS AND PINTUCKS — ALL INVALUABLE FOR SHAPING DRESSES AND OTHER GARMENTS.

TOP 10 DRESS STYLES

THESE TEN MOST POPULAR DRESS STYLES CAN BE ADAPTED TO MAKE HUNDREDS OF VARIATIONS TO SUIT ALL OCCASIONS, TASTES AND FASHIONS.

SHIFT DRESS

Casual, comfortable and easy to wear, a shift dress is loose-fitting and skims the figure to hide bumps and lumps. Shifts often have a wide neckline yoke and gathers or pleats at the front and back.

Fabrics: Make shifts in cottons, polyester, rayon, crushed velvet, silky satin and stretch knits.

Special techniques: Making facings, gathers and pleats

Ease of sewing: Easy

WRAP DRESS

Flattering for all figure types, a wrap dress is particularly good for full-busted figures. The V-neckline of a wrap takes the eye down, giving an elongated silhouette. Smaller busted women should avoid wrap dresses, which can gape, or wear them over a little camisole.

Fabrics: Made in cotton or silk jersey, a wrap can be practical or luxurious and dressy.

Special techniques: Working with knit fabrics, stabilizing seams

Ease of sewing: Easy–intermediate

PINAFORE/JUMPER

A classic style, the pinafore can be quick to make and easy to wear. The style is usually sleeveless, designed to be worn over a top or blouse. Pinafores can be loose and pleated or semi-fitted with darts.

Fabrics: Make them in medium-weight fabric, such as wools, gabardine, worsteds and double knit jersey.

Special techniques: Lining a bodice, making pleats, inserting pockets (optional), making facings

Ease of sewing: Intermediate

HALTER-NECK DRESS

This sleeveless dress has straps that tie behind the neck. Halter-neck dresses often have an empire line to give support under the bust, but can also have a wide midriff band to define the waist. Halters are good for sundresses or evening wear. Those with fuller figures will need a halterneck bra.

Fabrics: A wide range will suit halters, depending on the occasion, from silks, satins, and velvets for evening to cotton and cotton/polyester mixes for day.

Special techniques: Adding straps, inserting zippers, making pleats and gathers

Ease of sewing: Easy–intermediate

FITTED SHELL DRESS

The most classic of dresses, a fitted shell usually has a round or bateau neckline, and is darted front and back with a side or back zipper. Figure hugging and chic, a shell dress can have a straight or a full pleated skirt. The look is ideal for evening wear.

Fabrics: Make shell dresses in silks, satins, lace, brocade and duchess satin.

Special techniques: Inserting darts and zippers, stabilizing seams

Ease of sewing: Intermediate–advanced

PRINCESS LINE DRESS

Defined by the seams running from mid-armhole to hem, this is the easiest style to fit at the bust, waist or hip because of the extra seaming. A princess line provides a flattering fit for all figures.

Fabrics: Cottons, wool, worsteds, gabardine or polyester are suitable. Be careful with prints as the extra seaming will interrupt the design. Choose plain or all-over prints.

Special techniques: Fitting with seaming, inserting zippers

Ease of sewing: Easy–intermediate

BIAS-CUT DRESS

Figure skimming to fit where it touches, a bias cut is easy to wear, but can reveal lumps and bumps! Often made without fastenings because the bias fabric will stretch easily, a bias-cut dress is easy to make. It will have fluidity and so is great for active wear.

Fabrics: Silky polyesters, chiffon or georgette work well for bias cuts.

Special techniques: Cutting on the bias, making facings, bias-binding seams

Ease of sewing: Easy

EMPIRE LINE DRESS

An empire line dress has a high waist or underbust seam from which the skirt section falls, skimming the waist and hips. It's a good style for those without a definite waist or with a smaller bust; however, it can make big-busted women look pregnant! An empire line can be incorporated into a pinafore or simple shift, work with straps on a sundress or add detail to a halter-neck dress.

Fabrics: You can use a wide range from wools or gabardine to cotton, linen, silk and taffeta.

Special techniques: Inserting zippers, making darts

Ease of sewing: Easy–intermediate

SUNDRESS

Sleeveless, short sleeve or strappy, a sundress can be a combination of other dress styles, including empire line, bias cut, halter neck or pinafore features. The essential element is that it should be suitable for hot weather.

Fabrics: Use easily laundered fabrics such as linen, cotton, batik or polyester.

Special techniques: Adding straps, binding armholes, making pleats, inserting zippers

Ease of sewing: Easy–intermediate

SHIRTWAISTER

This traditional work dress resembles a shirt with a collar, cuffed sleeves and buttoned through front. It can be straight or flared with an A-line skirt. Practical and classic, it can be brought up-to-date with a wide belt and chunky accessories.

Fabrics: Crisp cottons, linens or polyester mixes are ideal for shirtwaisters.

Special techniques: Adding collars and cuffs, making buttonholes and plackets

Ease of sewing: Advanced

DARTS

DARTS ARE USED TO SHAPE A GARMENT AT THE BUST, WAIST OR SHOULDERS. THEY FOLD OUT THE FABRIC, REMOVING THE EXCESS IN SOME AREAS, SUCH AS AROUND THE WAIST, AND TAPERING TO THE POINT OF THE DART TO ALLOW FULLNESS. CORRECTLY MADE AND POSITIONED, DARTS HELP THE FABRIC TO MOULD TO THE BODY CONTOURS AND THEY IMPROVE THE FIT OF THE GARMENT.

DARTS FOR DIFFERENT PURPOSES

SINGLE DARTS

Most darts are single and used to shape at the shoulder or bust. They are wider at the outer edge and taper to nothing within the garment.

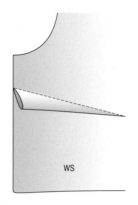

FIGURE 1 A SINGLE DART TAPERS TO A POINT, FOLDING OUT MOST FABRIC AT THE SEAM END.

DOUBLE-ENDED DARTS

Double-ended darts are used to shape the front and back waistline of a dress. Effectively two single darts joined at the widest part in the centre, they taper to nothing at both ends. In order to take in a considerable amount of fabric, there may be two or four at the front and two or four at the back, on each side of the centre.

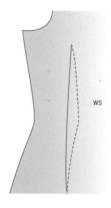

FIGURE 2 A DOUBLE-ENDED DART TAPERS AT BOTH ENDS, FOLDING OUT MOST FABRIC IN THE MIDDLE.

WORKING WITH A PATTERN

Dart placement and stitching lines are included on commercial patterns and need to be transferred to the wrong side of fabric sections before cutting out the fabric. At the same time, you can make any adjustments needed for a more accurate fit (see pp. 38–41).

Flirty fitted shell dress
The striking pattern and modern colours of this cotton-mix make a very striking dress. The darts at the bust add shaping to the bodice. The dress also features a gathered skirt (see p. 61), a back zipper (see p. 66), a lined bodice (see p. 55) and button loops (see p. 69).

❀ **The pattern is New Look 6799.**

WORKING WITHOUT A PATTERN

If you are working without a commercial pattern, darts can be added to a garment quite easily.

For skirts, add single darts to the front and back sections from the waist to just above the hip. To determine how wide the dart should be, divide the difference between the waist and hip measurements by four (for two darts at the front and two at the back). If the resulting measurement is more than 1½in (4cm), make six equal darts instead, two at the front and four at the back.

On a top, add single darts to provide bust shaping. Position one in each front side seam, just below the armhole, taking it to within 1in (2.5cm) of the bust point. For fuller busts and to give extra fitting, it is advisable to have a second long dart from the waist up to just below the bust point.

MARKING AND MAKING SINGLE DARTS

1 Mark the dart position on the fabric where required, marking the two widest points and the tapered end. For long darts, also mark midway along each stitch line.

FIGURE 3 MARK THE DART POSITION AT LEAST AT THE WIDEST AND POINTED ENDS.

2 Fold the fabric right sides together, bringing the two marked points together at the fabric edge and folding through the inner point. Pin in place. Chalk a line from the outer mark to the point.

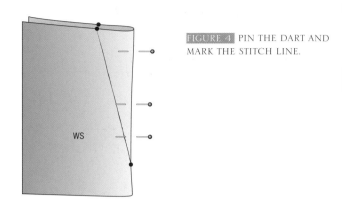

FIGURE 4 PIN THE DART AND MARK THE STITCH LINE.

3 Stitch along the marked line, from the widest end to the dart point, making the last few stitches right at the fold. To fasten off, stitch on the spot or leave threat tails to knot. Do not back stitch as that may cause a ridge.

4 Press the dart from both sides, away from the centre on vertical darts or downwards on horizontal darts, such as bust darts.

EXPERT TIP
If pressing a dart for a full bust, press the dart over a dressmaker's ham or tightly rolled towel to help shape the fabric.

WORKING WITH HEAVYWEIGHT FABRIC

If pressed to one side, a dart in a heavyweight fabric would be rather bulky. To avoid excessive bulk, cut open the dart along the fold once it has been stitched. Cut close to the tapered end and press each side open.

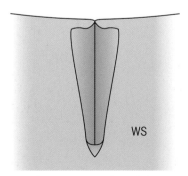

FIGURE 5 CUT ALONG THE FOLD AND PRESS THE DART FLAT.

EXPERT TIP
Dab a spot of fray check at the tapered end of darts in fabrics that fray easily.

MAKING DOUBLE-ENDED DARTS

Double-ended darts are ideal for shaping waistlines and can be used to take in a considerable amount of fabric.

1 Mark and fold the dart in a similar way to steps 1 and 2 for single darts.

2 Begin to stitch from the centre/widest part of the dart to one tapered point. Repeat from the centre to the other point.

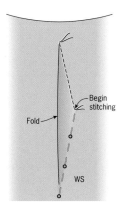

FIGURE 6 STITCH FROM THE CENTRE TO THE POINT.

3 To help the dart curve into the body as it is meant to, clip the folded fabric at the centre/widest part of the dart on the wrong side of the garment. Then press the dart towards the centre of the garment.

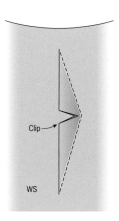

FIGURE 7 CLIP ACROSS THE FOLD AT THE CENTRE OF THE DART.

EXPERT TIP

To obtain a very close fit, you could curve the stitching line of the dart. If you wish to allow slightly more fullness for a fuller bust, for example, start and finish the stitch line at the usual points, but curve it slightly in towards the fold of fabric. Curve the stitch line outwards away from the fold to take more fabric into the dart to give a snugger fit, for instance, into a hollow back.

MAKING COUTURE DARTS

Couture darts are stitched in the same manner as ordinary double-ended darts, but incorporate an additional layer of fabric. This allows the same amount of bulk to be pressed to each side of the dart seam, giving a smoother appearance on the right side of the garment.

1 Mark and fold the dart in a similar way to steps 1 and 2 for double-ended darts.

2 Start to stitch the dart from the centre to one tapered point and onto the remnant. Repeat from the centre to the other point.

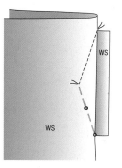

FIGURE 8 PLACE A REMNANT OF FABRIC UNDER THE DART.

3 Fold the remnant away from the dart and cut away the excess, leaving the remnant level with the folded edge of the dart.

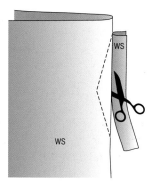

FIGURE 9 FOLD THE FABRIC AND CUT AWAY CLOSE TO THE STITCHING.

4 Clip the centre/widest part of the dart, across the folded fabric and the remnant. Then press the dart to one side and the remnant to the other. This gives the dart a flatter appearance on the right side, like a seam, rather than having bulk on only one side.

DARTING LININGS

When making linings for skirts and trousers, rather than making a waist dart in the lining fabric to match one in the main fabric, take a small pleat the same size as the dart at the edge of the garment. This will provide more ease in the lining fabric and avoid the bulk of two dart folds on top of each other.

When making double darts for dresses, press the main fabric dart towards the centre and the lining dart towards the side seam to even out the bulk.

PLEATS, TUCKS AND PIN TUCKS

PLEATS, TUCKS AND PIN TUCKS ARE FORMED BY FOLDS IN THE FABRIC. THIS MAY BE TO FOLD OUT EXCESS FABRIC, TO PROVIDE SHAPING OR AS A DESIGN FEATURE. ADDITIONAL FABRIC IS NEEDED TO CREATE THESE FOLDS AND, OF COURSE, THE PRECISE AMOUNT DEPENDS ON THE NUMBER AND SIZE OF THE PLEATS OR TUCKS.

PLEATS

There are three types of pleat – knife-edge, box and inverted.

KNIFE-EDGE PLEATS

These straight pleats all face the same direction, lapping right over left or left over right.

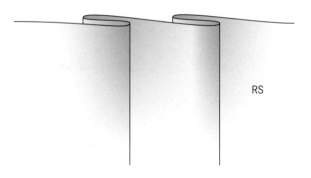

KNIFE-EDGE PLEATS

BOX PLEATS

A box pleat comprises two pleats, turned away from each other to form a straight flat panel in the centre.

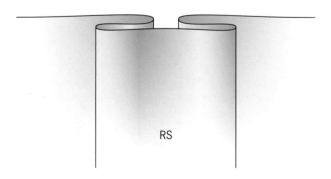

BOX PLEAT

Perfectly pleated pinafore

This pinafore dress looks just the business in pure wool herringbone. It features an inverted pleat at the centre front with two knife-edge pleats on each side and a single inverted pleat at the centre back. This style also has in-seam pockets (see p. 92), a centred zipper (see p. 71) and bias taped armholes (see p. 102–103).

❀ **The pattern is Simplicity 2848.**

INVERTED PLEATS

An inverted pleat has two pleats turned towards each other to form an opening at the centre. Kick pleats are a variation of the inverted pleat and may have the underlay section cut from contrast fabric to add design detail.

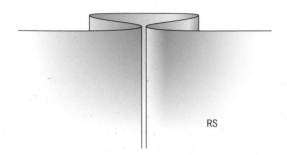

INVERTED PLEAT

WORKING WITH A PATTERN

If you are using a commercial pattern, the extra fabric has already been allowed for and markings, showing how the pleats are folded and formed, are incorporated on the pattern pieces. Transfer the markings to the fabric before cutting out.

WORKING WITHOUT A PATTERN

If you are working without a commercial pattern, or you wish to add pleats to a plain garment, first calculate how wide the folded pleat will be and then double the measurement. For instance, a folded pleat that is 1in (2.5cm) wide will take 2in (5cm) of fabric. This is the extra fabric you will need for the one pleat, so for more pleats add all the pleat allowances for each garment piece.

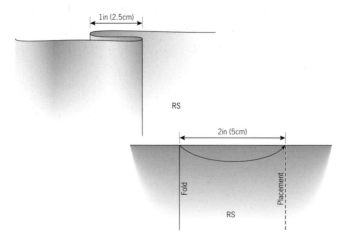

FIGURE 1 CALCULATE THE EXTRA FABRIC NEEDED FOR ONE PLEAT BY DOUBLING THE PLEAT WIDTH.

EXPERT TIP

Make a pleat template from stiff card, cut to the width of the whole pleat allowance. Mark 'placement' on one edge and 'fold' along the other.

MARKING AND FORMING PLEATS

1 Mark the fabric to be pleated using a card template or transfer the pleat markings from the pattern tissue to the fabric. If the pleats are to remain unpressed, mark the pleat lines down from the top edge by just 2–4in (5–10cm). If they are to be part stitched or pressed, mark them for a further 4in (10cm). For crisp pressed pleats, mark the whole length of the pleat.

SEWING SENSE

Use different coloured chalks for the fold and placement lines so it is easy to see which is which, or mark the fold with a cross and the placement with a straight line.

2 Carefully fold the pleats, taking the fold over to the placement line along the entire length of the pleat and keeping the upper edges even. Pin and baste the pleats in place along the top edge. Press the pleats carefully with a press cloth to avoid leaving fold imprints on the fabric.

3 Keep the pleats in place by machine stitching across the top within the seam allowance.

4 To maintain crisp pleats all the way down the length, work from the wrong side to machine stitch close to the inner fold of fabric.

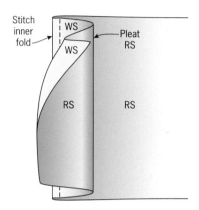

FIGURE 2 MACHINE STITCH ALONG THE EDGE OF THE INNER FOLD.

EXPERT TIP

To maintain neat, crisp pleats, fuse slotted waistbanding on the wrong side of the pleat with the slots along the foldline.

REGULAR TUCKS

Tucks are generally smaller than pleats and sewn in place all the way along the folded edge. Not only do tucks add decorative detail, they can also be used to help with fit.

Tucks are usually formed in groups along the straight grain, parallel with selvages or warp fabric threads. Generally, horizontal tucks are pressed downwards, while vertical tucks are pressed away from the centre.

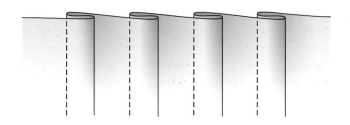

TUCKS

As with pleats, tucks take up extra fabric so it is important that they are measured, marked and sewn very accurately. Even tiny inaccuracies have a big impact; for instance, if you are making 12 tucks across a top and each takes ¾in (2cm) of fabric, an ⅛in error per tuck can mean 3in (7.5cm) difference in the size of the finished garment.

FORMING TUCKS

1 As with pleats, the easiest way to mark tucks onto fabric if you are not using a commercial pattern is to create a card template (see the Expert Tip on p. 84, but also incorporate the space between tucks on your template). This will ensure that you mark all the fold lines, placement lines and spaces accurately. If you are using a commercial pattern, the tuck markings will be printed on the pattern and need to be transferred to the fabric. Use a chalk pencil or other fade-away pen to transfer the markings to the right side of the fabric at the top and bottom of the tuck.

EXPERT TIP

To mark the fabric quickly for full length tucks, clip the seam allowance with scissors at the top and bottom of the tucks, marking fold lines with a wedge-shape and placement lines with a straight cut.

2 Fold the fabric one tuck at a time, pinning it in place at the top and bottom and, for a long tuck, at intervals down the length.

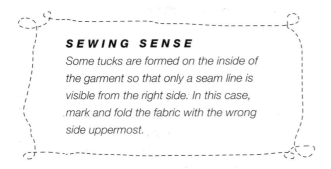

SEWING SENSE

Some tucks are formed on the inside of the garment so that only a seam line is visible from the right side. In this case, mark and fold the fabric with the wrong side uppermost.

3 Place the tuck under the presser foot and sew from top to bottom, stitching along the placement line so that the fold to the right is free.

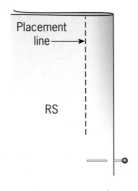

Placement line →

RS

FIGURE 3 STITCH ALONG THE PLACEMENT LINE THROUGH TWO LAYERS OF FABRIC.

4 Fold the next tuck and stitch it as before. It is easier to work from left to right, folding and stitching the left tuck first, then moving across to the next tuck to the right.

EXPERT TIP

Stitch tucks on garment sections before cutting out the pieces as lots of tucks will reduce the width of the fabric section.

PIN TUCKS

Pin tucks are very narrow tucks formed by taking small folds of fabric. They can be corded (with a length of cord laid inside the fold) to make them more prominent. An alternative method of creating pin tucks is to use a twin needle in conjunction with a pin tuck presser foot.

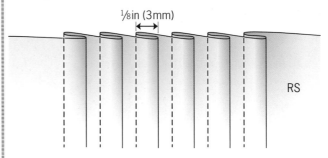

⅛in (3mm)

RS

PIN TUCKS

MAKING REGULAR PIN TUCKS

These straight pleats all face the same direction, lapping right over left or left over right.

1 Mark and fold the pin tuck top and bottom as for regular tucks (see steps 1 and 2 on pp. 85-86). Press the folds in place.

2 Position one tuck under the presser foot so that the fold is to the right. Move the needle position to the far right so that you can stitch close to the edge – ⅛–¼in (3–6mm) is ideal. If available, use a ¼in (6mm) foot or edge stitch foot.

3 Press the tuck and continue to make the rest in turn.

TWIN NEEDLE PIN TUCKS

Twin needle pin tucks are quick and easy to form using the right tools. Pin tuck feet have three, five or seven grooves on the underside into which the fabric runs. They often come in packs of two, one foot with larger grooves for heavier weight fabrics and the other with smaller grooves for lightweight fabrics.

PIN TUCK FEET

Use a twin needle with a small gap between the needles on lightweight fabric and a slightly wider gap between the needles for heavier weight fabrics. For example, a ⅝in (1.6mm) gap and 10 (70) needle is perfect for lightweight fabrics, while a 1½in

(4 mm) gap and 14 (90) is better suited to wools. If sewing jersey, use a ballpoint or stretch needle.

The twin needles use two top threads and stitch on each side of the centre groove in the pin tuck foot. The single bobbin thread zigzags underneath between the top threads, pulling the fabric up a little to form a raised tuck that feeds through the groove.

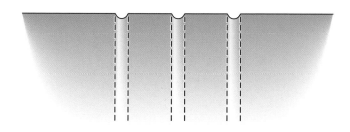

TWIN NEEDLE TUCKS

MAKING TWIN NEEDLE PIN TUCKS

1 Mark the position of the first tuck by drawing a chalk line along the entire length.

2 Attach the pin tuck foot and change to a twin needle. Select the centre needle position. Increase the tension to approximately 7 on the tension dial.

3 Thread two top threads through the thread path and use a matching thread in the bobbin.

EXPERT TIP
To avoid the top threads tangling, place one clockwise on the spindle and the other anticlockwise.

4 Position the fabric under the presser foot with the marked line in the centre of the foot so the needles will stitch on each side of the line. Stitch the tuck to the end.

5 Move the fabric so the first tuck sits in a groove to right or left of centre and stitch the next tuck in the same direction. You could move the tuck into the groove next to the stitching hole or leave one groove or any other spacing you prefer between tucks. Continue, to stitch a row of perfectly formed, evenly spaced tucks.

CORDED PIN TUCKS
These are more pronounced and firmer than regular pin tucks because a length of fine cord is fed under the centre groove on the presser foot as the tuck is stitched.

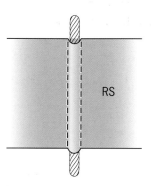

SEWING SENSE
Try out tuck composition on a fabric remnant to see whether you want the tucks very close together or evenly spaced a groove width apart, or to use the edge of the presser foot as a guide.

CORDED PIN TUCKS

Some manufacturers offer a separate throat plate cover or guide to attach to the throat plate to help make raised pin tucks. Used with the pin tuck foot, the cord is fed through the guide, keeping it in line with the centre groove on the presser foot as the twin needles stitch the tuck. If a cord guide is not available, guide the cord by hand as you sew.

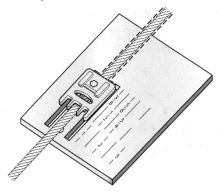

CORD GUIDE

EXPERT TIP
If you don't have a pin tuck foot, create corded tucks by sandwiching the cord in the fold and, using a zipper foot, stitch the tuck as close to the cord as possible.

BEST OF BOTTOMS

EVERY WOMAN NEEDS A SELECTION OF TROUSERS IN HER WARDROBE, RANGING FROM TRADITIONAL SMART STYLES FOR WORK TO COMFORTABLE SHORTS FOR HOLIDAYS. THIS ENSURES THAT YOU CAN CHOOSE FROM A RANGE OF COORDINATING PIECES TO SUIT EVERY OCCASION.

FASHION, AS WELL AS FUNCTIONALITY, DICTATES THAT STYLES VARY IN DESIGN, RESULTING IN A WIDE RANGE OF DETAILING AND DIFFERENT LEG WIDTHS AND WAIST HEIGHTS. HOWEVER, WHATEVER THE DESIGN, MOST TROUSERS HAVE A FLY-ZIP AND POCKETS OF SOME SORT, AND THIS CHAPTER SHOWS YOU HOW TO INSERT BOTH.

TOP 10 TROUSER SHAPES

THERE IS A TROUSER SHAPE TO SUIT ALL FIGURES, SO TAKE A LOOK AT THESE FAVOURITE SILHOUETTES AND PICK THE ONE TO SUIT YOU.

TRADITIONAL FLY-FRONT TROUSERS

Usually with hip-line/side-slant pockets and a waistband, the traditional trouser shape is straight legged and smart to wear with a fitted blouse and/or with a jacket as part of a suit. It is kinder to a pear-shaped figure to leave the pockets out.

Fabrics: Gabardine, flannel, woollens and wool mixes, linens

Special techniques: Inserting hip-line pockets, fly-front zipper and waistbanding

Ease of sewing: Intermediate–advanced

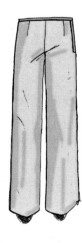

STRAIGHT-LEGGED TROUSERS WITH SIDE ZIP

This is a more flattering silhouette for those with large tummies as there is no additional bulk in the front. A faced waist, rather than a waistband, is good for short-waisted figures. Darts at the front and back will aid fitting through the hips and waist.

Fabrics: Gabardine, flannel, woollens and wool mixes, linens; cottons for summer wear

Special techniques: Inserting lapped zipper and darts, adding facings

Ease of sewing: Intermediate

WIDE LEGGED TROUSERS

Flattering for fuller figures, this shape is fitted to the hip and then flares out to the wide hem edge, thus balancing wider hips. This style can have a fly front or side lapped zipper, a waistband or facing, depending on your personal choice.

Fabrics: Flannel, gabardine; crepe-backed satins and medium-weight silks for evenings; medium to heavy cottons for summer.

Special techniques: Inserting zipper, waistbanding or facings

Ease of sewing: Intermediate

PALAZZO TROUSERS

Casual, easy make and wear trousers for sport or leisure, these usually have a drawstring or elasticated waist. They may have hip-line or side-seam pockets and can be straight or wide legged.

Fabrics: Cottons, stretch knits, silks, polyesters

Special techniques: Adding drawstring casing and pockets

Ease of sewing: Easy-intermediate

BOOT LEGGED TROUSER

This is a flattering style for all figures and is a common style for jeans or trouser suits. The trousers flare out from the knee to the hem.

Fabrics: Medium-weight fabrics with closely woven structure such as denim, flannel, worsteds, gabardine

Special techniques: Inserting zipper and waistbanding

Ease of sewing: Intermediate

CAPRI PANTS

Cropped to mid-calf or just below the knee, these are slim-legged trousers with side slits at the hem. Generally a smart-casual style, they can have a fly-front or side zipper, a waistband or faced waist, depending on personal preference.

Fabrics: Cottons, cotton sateen, satin, glazed cotton, gabardine

Special techniques: Making side slits, inserting zipper, waistbanding or facing

Ease of sewing: Intermediate

SKINNY FIT TROUSERS

Figure-hugging and close-fitting on the legs, this is a style that only flatters slim figures! Usually associated with jeans, skinny fit trousers are frequently worn tucked into heeled boots to give a longer leg. If you've got good legs but wider hips, wear skinny fit trousers with a tunic top that covers the thighs.

Fabrics: This style needs fabric with some stretch — denim mixed with Lycra® or elastaline, cotton mix, etc.

Special techniques: Fitting trousers, inserting hip-line pockets, fly-front zipper and waistbanding

Ease of sewing: Intermediate–advanced

CULOTTES/GAUCHES

Wide-legged, long-line shorts or cropped trousers with the fullness of an A-line skirt, culottes or gauches can be a smart alternative to trousers or skirt for office wear.

Fabrics: Medium-weight closely woven fabrics such as gabardine, worsteds, linen-look

Special techniques: Inserting waistbanding, fly-front zipper, darts or pleats

Ease of sewing: Intermediate

CARGO PANTS

These are casual sporty trousers, usually with a number of pockets including patched cargo pockets on the side of the trouser leg, shaped patch pockets and back pockets. They can have a drawstring waist or a waistband and occasionally have a drawstring hem line too.

Fabrics: Glazed cotton, heavyweight cottons, double-knit jersey

Special techniques: Adding pockets and drawstring casing, inserting waistbanding and fly-front zipper

Ease of sewing: Intermediate

SHORTS

This term covers a diverse range of styles and lengths, depending on the use. They can be straight-legged above-knee city shorts for smart wear, Bermuda or boxer styles for holiday and sport, or walking shorts with a wider hem. Shorts are basically any trouser styles that finish above the knee.

Fabrics: Gabardine, linen-look, heavyweight cotton, raw silk for smart shorts; cottons and cotton mixes, linen-look, stretch knits for casual shorts

Special techniques: Making an elasticated waist, inserting darts, facings and fly-front zipper.

Ease of sewing: Easy–intermediate

POCKETS

THERE ARE DIFFERENT STYLES OF
POCKET RANGING FROM SIMPLE PATCH
VARIETIES TO CONCEALED IN-SEAM
POCKETS, AS WELL AS THE FRONT
HIP-LINE POCKETS USUALLY ASSOCIATED
WITH SMART TROUSERS AND JEANS.
THEY CAN BE ADDED TO ANY GARMENT
AND MADE FROM THE SAME OR
CONTRAST FABRIC.

PATCH POCKETS

Patch pockets can be virtually any shape although traditionally they are square or rectangle. They can be made from the same fabric as the garment, a contrast fabric as a design detail, lined or unlined. Once formed, the pocket is top stitched to the garment.

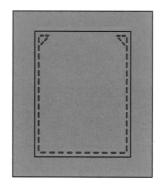 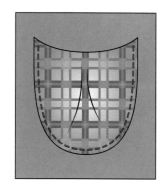

DIFFERENT TYPES OF
PATCH POCKETS

MAKING SELF-LINED PATCH POCKETS

This is the simplest type of patch pocket to make.

1 Cut the fabric for the pocket twice the length required plus $5/_8$in (1.5cm) seam allowances all the way around. Fold the fabric in half, right sides together. The fold will become the top of the pocket.

2 Stitch the side and bottom seams, leaving an opening for turning in the bottom edge. Clip the corners at angles.

3 Turn the pocket through the opening. Press and slip stitch the opening closed. If desired, top stitch ¼in (6mm) from the fold to create a crisp top.

Palazzo trousers

Wide-legged, palazzo pants are wonderfully flattering. Those shown have a side lapped zip, hip-line pockets and a waistband with belt carriers through which a contrast fabric tie can be fed.

❀ **The pattern is New Look 6896.**

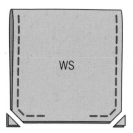

FIGURE 1 STITCH AND TRIM THE SEAMS AROUND THE POCKET.

4 Position the pocket on the garment. Then stitch it in place, ⅛in (3mm) from the edge. Start at the top of one side by stitching a triangle. Continue stitching down the side, across the bottom, and up the other side, finishing with another triangle.

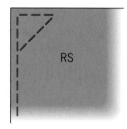

FIGURE 2 STITCH A TRIANGLE AT THE TOP OF THE POCKET TO ENSURE THAT IT DOESN'T RIP AWAY FROM THE GARMENT.

MAKING LINED PATCH POCKETS

If the main fabric is heavyweight or bulky (such as coatings or fleece), a lining is preferable to self-lining.

1 Mark out the pocket size on the main fabric and the lining. Then add ⅝in (1.5cm) seam allowances at the sides and the bottom edge, and 1¼in (3cm) on the top edge.

2 Stitch the main fabric and the lining right sides together along the top edge, taking a ¼in (6mm) seam and leaving an opening for turning in the middle of the seam.

3 Mark a foldline on the main fabric 1in (2.5cm) from the seam and turn the pocket top towards the lining along the foldline

4 Pin and stitch the side and bottom seams, including the folded down top in the stitching. Trim the seam allowances, clipping the corners at an angle.

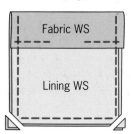

FIGURE 3 STITCH AND TRIM THE SEAMS, STITCHING DOWN THE FOLDED TOP.

5 Turn the pocket through the opening. Press and slip stitch the opening closed. Position the pocket on the garment and attach it as in step 4, left, for self-lined pockets.

IN-SEAM POCKETS

This type of pocket can also be made from the fashion fabric, or from lining to avoid too much bulk in the hip area. In-seam pockets are made from two pieces, attached to the front and back garment sections before the side seams of the garment are stitched.

MAKING IN-SEAM POCKETS

1 If you are working with a commercial pattern, pocket pieces will be included. If not, loosely draw around the hand, allowing room for movement and seam allowances and adding a straight edge at the wrist end, which will be attached to the side seam of the garment.

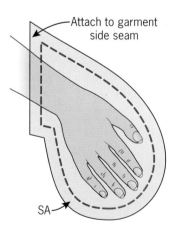

Attach to garment side seam

SA

FIGURE 4 REMEMBER TO ADD SEAM ALLOWANCES TO THE BASIC POCKET SHAPE.

2 Cut two pieces from the main fabric or lining.

3 Pin each piece, right sides together, to the side seam of the front or back garment pieces, approximately 3in (7.5cm) below the waist edge. Sew, taking a ⅝in (1.5cm) seam allowance. Press.

4 Pin the front and back garment sections, right sides together, matching the pocket placement and with the pocket extending beyond the seam. Stitch from the waist edge to ⅝in (1.5cm) from the pocket seam, pivot and then sew around the pocket shape, stitching the pocket sections together. Once back on the garment seam line, pivot the work and stitch the remainder of the seam.

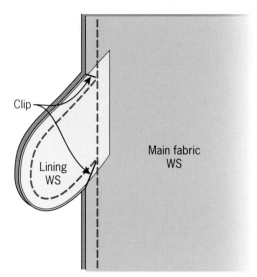

FIGURE 5 STITCH THE SIDE SEAMS AND AROUND THE POCKET, AND THEN CLIP ACROSS THE SEAM ALLOWANCES ABOVE AND BELOW THE POCKET.

5 Neaten the edges, clipping into the angle at the top and bottom of the pocket. Then press the seam allowances of the pocket towards the pocket shape before pressing the pocket towards the front of the garment.

HIP-LINE POCKETS

These are also known as side slant pockets. They have a shaped front opening and are usually found on traditional trousers or jeans. They are a two-part pocket with a facing and a pocket bag/back. The facing, cut from lining or the main fabric, is attached to the angled trouser front. The pocket back is attached to the side seam and then waistband as it forms part of the top edge of the trousers.

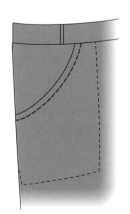

HIPLINE POCKET

EXPERT TIP

Leave pockets out if their inclusion spoils the silhouette or adds unwanted bulk to curvy figures.

MAKING HIP-LINE POCKETS

1 Reinforce the opening edge of the pocket facing by stay stitching just within the seam allowance or fusing edge tape to the seam allowance. Do the same for the garment edge.

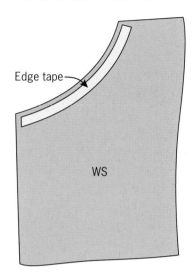

FIGURE 6 REINFORCE THE POCKET FACE WITH EDGE TAPE OR STAY STITCHING.

2 With right sides together, stitch the facing to the garment edge. Then grade the seam allowances to reduce bulk, press them towards the facing and under stitch (see p. 25).

3 Turn the facing to the inside, press again and, if desired, top stitch close to the edge.

4 Keeping the garment out of the way, match and machine stitch the side and bottom edges of the pocket facing to the pocket back, right sides together. Neaten the raw edges and press.

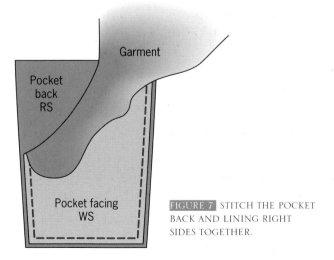

FIGURE 7 STITCH THE POCKET BACK AND LINING RIGHT SIDES TOGETHER.

5 Pin the back and front garment sections together, catching the side edge of the pocket into the seam, and stitch. The top of the pocket back can then be attached to the waistband as part of the top edge of the trousers.

FLY-FRONT ZIPPERS

THE FLY-FRONT IS A VARIATION ON THE LAPPED ZIPPER AND HAS AN ADDITIONAL FLY BEHIND THE ZIPPER. IT'S THE TRADITIONAL METHOD USED FOR TROUSERS AND JEANS. LADIES' FLY-FRONTS ARE INSERTED WITH THE RIGHT SIDE OF THE FLAP OVER THE LEFT. IT IS ESSENTIAL THAT THE CORRECT LENGTH OF ZIPPER IS USED AS THE TOP STITCHING GOES ACROSS THE BOTTOM OF THE FLY-FRONT AND IF THE NEEDLE HITS THE ZIPPER TEETH, IT MAY BREAK.

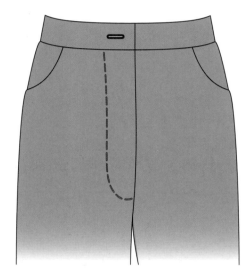

FLY-FRONT TROUSERS

Straight trousers

Straight-legged trousers with a fly-front are a classic capsule wardrobe style. Those shown here have a contoured waistband that is designed to sit comfortably ½in (1.3cm) below the waist. The inside of the waistband is neatened with the serger, rather than finishing with bias binding. A hook and eye keeps the top of the waistband in place.

❧ **The pattern is Simplicity 2860.**

INSERTING A FLY-FRONT ZIPPER

1 First make the fly section, approximately 4in (10cm) wide and 1in (2.5cm) longer than the zipper. Fold the fabric in half, wrong sides together, and sew the edges together. Neaten the seam allowance and set the fly section to one side.

FIGURE 1 MAKE A DOUBLE-SIDED FLY SECTION.

2 On the trousers, with right sides together, machine stitch from the base of the zipper position to the crotch. Then baste the zipper opening closed. Neaten the seam allowances separately and then press them open.

3 With the trousers wrong side up, place the zipper face down with the teeth centred over the basted seam line. Pin and stitch the left side of the zipper tape to the seam allowance only, stitching approximately ¼in (6mm) from the edge of the tape.

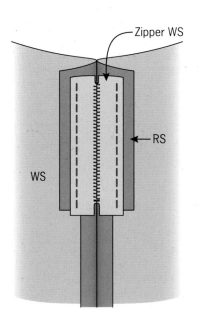

FIGURE 2 POSITION THE ZIPPER CENTRALLY OVER THE UNDERSIDE OF THE SEAM LINE AND STITCH THE LEFT ZIPPER TAPE TO THE SEAM ALLOWANCE.

4 Gently pull the right zipper tape over in line with the right edge of the other seam allowance and then pin through all the thicknesses. Turn the trousers right side uppermost and check for wrinkles, repinning neatly if necessary.

5 Chalk mark a stitching guideline and then top stitch from the seam line at the base of the zipper up to the waistline. Remove any basting and try out the zipper.

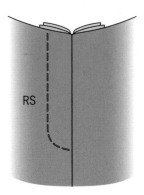

FIGURE 3 STITCH THE ZIPPER TO THE MAIN FABRIC.

6 Working from the inside of the garment, pin and then stitch the fly in position behind the zipper, with the neatened edge of the fly in line with the edge of the seam allowance, stitching it to the seam allowance only.

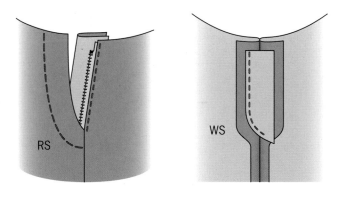

FIGURE 4 STITCH THE FLY IN POSITION BEHIND THE ZIPPER.

TROUSERS ALWAYS INCLUDE WEARING EASE SO THAT THEY
ARE COMFORTABLE TO WEAR WHATEVER YOU ARE DOING.

TOPS AND BLOUSES

AS PART OF A CAPSULE WARDROBE, A SELECTION OF TOPS IS ESSENTIAL. THESE CAN RANGE FROM SMART SHIRTS TO GYPSY-STYLE TUNICS OR SKIMPY CAMISOLES TO EDGE-TO-EDGE COVERINGS SUCH AS SHRUGS AND BOLEROS.

A COLLECTION OF DIFFERENT TOPS IN A RANGE OF FABRICS WILL EXTEND A FEW WARDROBE BASICS ENORMOUSLY. CHOOSE SILKS AND SATINS FOR EVENING WEAR, CRISP COTTONS OR POLYESTER FOR DAY OR LOVELY BOLD PRINTS FOR EASY TUNICS.

THE STYLE OF A BLOUSE OR TOP IS OFTEN DEFINED BY THE TYPE OF SLEEVES, STRAPS OR COLLAR IT FEATURES AND THIS CHAPTER SHOWS YOU HOW TO MAKE A WIDE RANGE OF VARIATIONS. BIAS BINDING AND BONING CAN ALSO ADD THAT ESSENTIAL DEFINING DETAIL AND ARE COVERED HERE TOO.

TOP 10 TOPS AND BLOUSES

BECAUSE OF THE WIDE RANGE OF DESIGNS WITHIN THIS GROUP THERE REALLY IS SOMETHING TO SUIT EVERY OCCASION AND FIGURE SHAPE.

TRADITIONAL BLOUSE OR SHIRT

Traditional blouses and shirts are very similar and both tend to have front button closures. However, a shirt usually also has a crisp collar and cuffs. A blouse has a softer look and may include design details such as a yoke, gathering or lace. Collar options range from traditional to granddad, Peter Pan or a bow and there is a huge variety of sleeve styles, from full length to short puffed sleeves, to choose from.

Fabrics: Lightweight fabrics with some body such as cotton shirtings, silks, satins, polyester mix

Special techniques: Making buttonholes, adding collar and cuffs, fitting sleeves

Ease of sewing: Easy–intermediate

GYPSY TUNIC BLOUSE TOP

This is a soft, free-flowing style usually with gathers or pleats to give fullness. It can be sleeveless or have sleeves, usually also featuring some gathering. It may have a yoked neckline, an added hip yoke or be free falling.

Fabrics: Cheesecloth, seersucker, cottons and cotton mixes, polyester, viscose

Special techniques: Making pleats and gathers, adding a faced yoke

Ease of sewing: Easy

KAFTAN TUNIC

An alternative, more stylised tunic top, this style traditionally has a detailed and shaped V-neckline with top stitching or trimming. Fuller sleeves and side slits on longer lengths add to the style. Generally loose fitting with bust darts, this top is great for holidays.

Fabrics: Cottons, batiks, lightweight linen

Sewing techniques: Adding darts, top stitching, fitting sleeves, attaching trimming

Ease of sewing: Easy

SHELL/VEST TOP

This is a very simply shaped top that can be loose or semi-fitted and is usually sleeveless. Semi-attached butterfly sleeves can cover the upper arms. The traditional shell top has only bust darts for shaping and a rounded neckline, but variations can include under-bust seaming, a V-neck line and front waist to bust darts.

Fabrics: Silks, satins, polyester, viscose, lightweight cottons, stretch knits

Sewing techniques: Making darts and side slits

Ease of sewing: Easy

BONED TOP

This is a very close fitting style, often without any straps as the boning along the seams gives shape and support. It is a style often used for evening and bridal wear, although brides usually add straps and occasionally even some sort of sleeve.

Fabrics: Silks, satins, lace, medium-weight cottons

Sewing techniques: Boning, inserting zippers, making rouleau loops

Ease of sewing: Intermediate

CAMISOLE

This is a strappy, lightweight top that can be worn under a jacket, dress or top, or on its own as a summer top. It can be bias cut, therefore needing no darts or closures, or semi-fitted and shaped. As a summer top, it might have empire seaming and a mock wrap. The straps are usually spaghetti or narrow.

Fabrics: Lightweight silks, satins, polyesters, chiffon, georgette, lace

Sewing techniques: Making rouleau loop straps, working with bias seams

Ease of sewing: Easy

WRAP TOP

Best made in a soft drapable fabric, a wrap top is a very flattering style for most figure shapes, particularly those with fuller busts. Wrap tops often have sleeves cut as one with the bodice sections or drop shoulders, kimono style, for easy sleeve insertion. This category also includes mock wraps, where a wrapped section is stitched in place on one side.

Fabrics: Jersey, knits; silks, satins or cottons for kimono styles

Sewing techniques: Sewing bias-cut seams, making bands

Ease of sewing: Easy

HALTER-NECK TOP

The straps are attached to the front of a halter-neck top and tied behind the neck, leaving the upper back open and strap free. The style of the front can vary greatly from being bias cut without shaping to having a drawstring neck edge, an empire line, a wrap front and even boning to add style and support.

Fabrics: Soft, fluid lightweight fabrics such as silks, polyesters, viscose, cottons, cotton mixes

Sewing techniques: Making ties or straps, top stitching

Ease of sewing: Easy

T-SHIRT

The traditional T-shirt has short sleeves and a round neckline, but there are many variations on the theme. These include a V-neckline, which is more flattering to fuller busted figures, a polo, cowl or bateau neck, and raglan sleeves, set in or batwing, which are cut from the same piece as the bodice.

Fabrics: Stretch knits, cotton jersey

Sewing techniques: Working with stretch knits, top stitching

Ease of sewing: Easy

BOLERO OR SHRUG

Neither of these styles have fastenings and often the sleeves are cut as one with the bodice. A bolero is cropped just below the bust, a cardigan-style top that meets edge to edge at the front, often with bias-bound edges. A shrug is shorter and smaller, covering the shoulders but without the edges meeting at the front.

Fabrics: Lace, silk, brocade, satin, raw silk, stretch knits

Sewing techniques: Bias binding

Ease of sewing: Easy

BIAS BINDING

BIAS BINDING IS A GREAT EDGING
OPTION TO NEATLY FINISH OFF THE
NECK, ARMHOLES AND FRONT EDGES
ON A BOLERO OR JACKET.

THE STRIPS ARE CUT ON THE BIAS SO
THAT THEY ARE EASIER TO SHAPE AND
MANIPULATE AROUND CURVES.
LIGHTWEIGHT FABRICS CAN BE BOUND
WITH NARROW BIAS BINDING, WHILE
HEAVIER WEIGHT COATINGS AND WOOLS
WILL NEED WIDER BIAS STRIPS.

BIAS BINDING

Available ready-made in different colours and widths, bias binding can
also be made from bias-cut strips of fabric of different widths using a
bias binding maker.

BIAS BINDING MAKER

It is often applied around the edges of garments to neaten and
strengthen them.

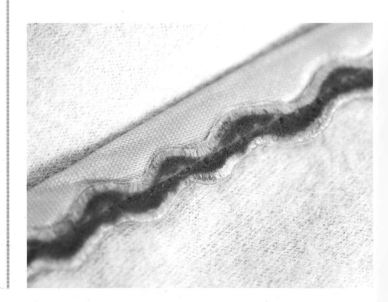

Bolero jacket

Add a bolero jacket to your wardrobe must-haves. It's quick to make and ideal to cover up on cooler days or when bare shoulders are a no-no. This one is made in wool jersey, lined with crinkled silk. The edges have been bound with bias binding, finished with rickrack, and top stitched in place.

❀ **The pattern is Simplicity 3921.**

MAKING BIAS BINDING

1 Find the true bias of the fabric by folding the cut edge up to the left selvage and then lightly press the fold. Unfold the fabric and, using the crease as a guideline, mark out the bias strips required so that each strip is twice the width of the finished binding.

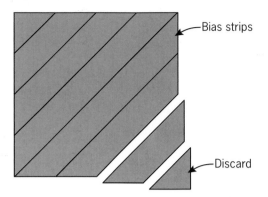

FIGURE 1 CUT OUT THE BIAS STRIPS ALONG PARALLEL DIAGONAL LINES.

2 Make long continuous strips of bias binding by joining shorter lengths together. Place the short ends of two strips together at right angles, right sides together, and stitch across diagonally starting at the top left corner and finishing at the bottom right corner. Press the seam allowances flat and open out the strip to form a continuous length.

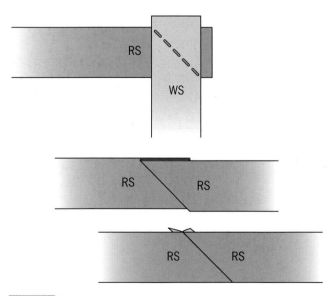

FIGURE 2 SEW THE STRIPS TOGETHER AT A 45-DEGREE ANGLE AND THEN PRESS THE SEAM FLAT.

3 Using the appropriately sized bias binding maker and working on an ironing board, feed one short end of the fabric strip into the tool and pull it out the other end, pressing with an iron as you pull the strip through, ready folded.

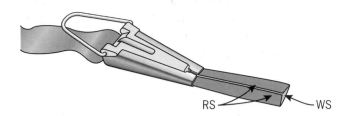

FIGURE 3 PRESS THE FOLDS AS YOU PULL THE BINDING FROM THE BINDING MAKER.

USING FOLDOVER BRAID

Foldover braid is an alternative to bias binding. It is also flexible as it is cut on the bias, but is folded just in two, usually slightly off-centre so one fold is deeper than the other. Pin the narrow fold to the front of the garment and fold the braid to the wrong side so that the inner edge overlaps the seaming, making it easier to stitch in the ditch from the front (see p. 25).

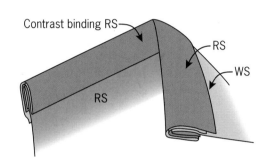

FIGURE 4 STITCH FOLDOVER BINDING IN THE DITCH FROM THE RIGHT SIDE, CATCHING IN THE WIDER FOLD OF BINDING ON THE UNDERSIDE OF THE GARMENT.

APPLYING BIAS BINDING

Make sure the binding is long enough to fit around the edge to be bound in one continuous piece.

1 Open out the bias binding and pin it to the garment edge, right sides together, so that the crease on the binding nearest to the garment edge is on the seam line. Stitch the binding in place. Trim the seam allowances and clip or notch around any curves.

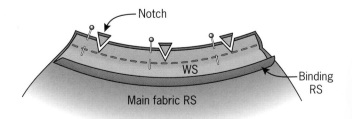

FIGURE 5 STITCH THE BINDING TO THE MAIN FABRIC ALONG THE CREASE NEAREST TO THE GARMENT EDGE.

2 Fold the binding to the wrong side so that the other folded edge of the binding sits just over the seam line and all the raw edges of the seam are encased. Either slip stitch the edge in place or stitch in the ditch from the front (see p. 25).

JOINING BIAS BINDING

On many bound edges, such as around a bolero, you will need to join the two ends of bias binding as neatly and in as inconspicuous a place as possible.

1 Start to pin the binding to the garment edge as in step 1, left. However, before stitching it in place, turn the raw pinned end to the wrong side.

2 Stitch the binding in place on the garment. Once back at the beginning, lay the other end of the binding over the neatened end, overlapping it by about ½in (1.3cm). Stitch the overlap down.

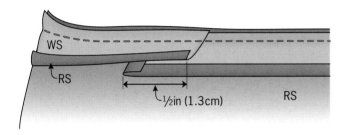

FIGURE 6 STITCH THE RAW END OF THE BINDING OVER THE FOLDED END.

3 Trim and clip or notch the seam as usual. Turn the binding to the wrong side so the neatened end is uppermost and finish the binding as usual.

SEWING SENSE

The easiest way to bind a right angle (as on a jacket front) is to bind the front edges and then bind the neck and hem edges separately, tucking the short raw ends to the inside and slip stitching them closed.

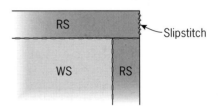

FIGURE 7 SLIP STITCH THE TURNED-UNDER RAW ENDS.

SLEEVES, CUFFS AND COLLARS

THE DIFFERENCE BETWEEN ONE
DESIGN AND ANOTHER IS OFTEN ALL
ABOUT THE DEFINING DETAILS. AS
WELL AS ADDING DECORATIVE EDGING
OR DECIDING ON STRAPS OR TIES, THE
CHOICE OF SLEEVES, CUFFS AND
COLLARS CAN TURN A SIMPLE
SILHOUETTE INTO A STYLISH DESIGN.

SLEEVES

While there are many different sleeve styles, there are only three main techniques for attaching them to a garment. A set-in sleeve is fitted into an armhole, a raglan sleeve generally has a diagonal seam from the neck to the underarm, and a kimono sleeve is cut as one with the bodice sections. There are, of course, variations on all of these, as well as choices to be made about length, fullness and cuff edge.

SETTING SLEEVES INTO ARMHOLES

This is probably the most common way to construct sleeves and includes many variations.

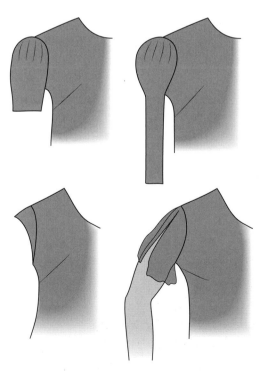

FOUR TYPES OF SET-IN SLEEVE

Simple blouse

This simple blouse, with its flat collar and puff sleeves finished with a continuous cuff, looks beautiful in embroidered cotton. It would also look great for evenings in silks, crepe de chine or double georgette.

✿ **The pattern is Simplicity 2732.**

Some set-in sleeves are made from one pattern piece; others, such as tailored sleeves, which may also have elbow shaping created with darts or ease stitches, are made from two pieces. Sleeve pattern pieces have notches at the front and back to match to similar notches on the front and back garment pieces. Usually there is a double notch at the back and a single notch on the front of the sleeve so that it is easy to match each sleeve to the correct side of the garment.

1 Stitch the underarm seam on the sleeve and on the shoulder and side seams on the garment. Press.

2 It is often necessary to ease stitch the sleeve head (the top curve of the sleeve) to fit it into the armhole. Machine stitch just within the seam allowance and then pull up the stitching to gather up the sleeve head until it fits the armhole, matching the notches and underarm seam.

3 With the sleeve right side out, slip it into the armhole of the garment, right sides together. Match the underarm seam with the garment side seam, the front and back notches and the top of the sleeve to the shoulder seam. Ease in any fullness still remaining.

4 Working with the sleeve uppermost, machine stitch it in place, starting at the underarm seam. With the sleeve uppermost, you can see the eased fabric and ensure that the gathers are only in the seam allowance to produce a smoothly fitted sleeve.

SETTING IN SLEEVES FLAT

Many set-in sleeves can be attached to the garment front and back before the side seams are stitched, making them easier to fit.

1 Join the garment front and back at the shoulder seams.

2 Ease the sleeve head as necessary. With right sides together, lay the sleeve on the garment front/back, matching the centre top of the sleeve to the shoulder seam and the notches to the front and back. Stitch the sleeve in place and neaten the raw edges. Press.

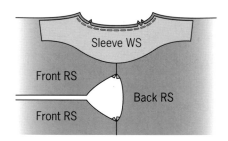

FIGURE 1 STITCH THE SLEEVE AND GARMENT FRONT/BACK TOGETHER AS TWO FLAT PIECES.

3 With right sides together, pin and stitch the underarm and side seams, starting at the cuff edge and pivoting underarm to stitch the side seams.

MAKING RAGLAN SLEEVES

Raglan sleeves may be cut as one with the front and back sections of the garment and thus have a seam along the top of the arm or may be cut as a one-piece sleeve, shaped either with diagonal seams from underarm to the neckline or with a dart along the shoulder line.

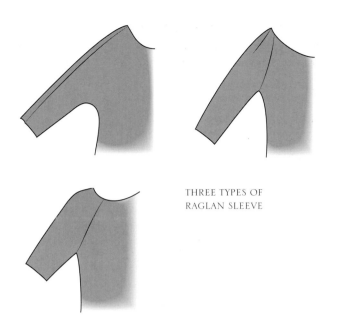

THREE TYPES OF
RAGLAN SLEEVE

1 Sew the sleeve to the front and back of the garment with right sides together.

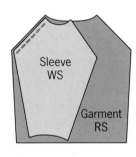

FIGURE 2 PIN AND STITCH THE UNDER ARM/NECK SEAM.

2 Place the front and back of the garment right sides together, matching up the seams. Pin and sew from the cuff edge to the garment hem in one pass. Repeat to the other side.

SEWING SENSE

Raglan sleeves are often used on sportswear and made in stretch fabric. To prevent the seams breaking when stretched, use a narrow zigzag or stretch stitch (see p. 23).

KIMONO SLEEVES

Kimono-style sleeves often have no seam joining the sleeves to the body of the garment as they are cut as one with the front and back sections. The sleeves can be long or short, boxy or more fitted. Drop shoulder sleeves are a variation, where a rectangular sleeve shape is attached to the garment sections before the underarm and side seams are sewn as one.

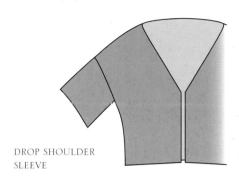

DROP SHOULDER
SLEEVE

INSERTING SHOULDER PADS

Although shoulder pads go in and out of fashion, they do add shape and drape to a sleeve head and give a better shoulder line. Ready-made shoulder pads are available and can be inserted as they are between the lining and the main fabric or they can be covered with lining fabric for insertion into an unlined top. Position the pads with the tapered thickness towards the neck and the wider edge at the shoulder. Slip stitch them to the shoulder seam allowance at the tapered edge and to the armhole seam at the front and back.

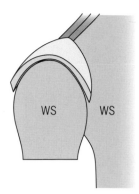

FIGURE 3 ALIGN THE WIDER EDGE OF THE SHOULDER PAD WITH THE SLEEVE HEAD SEAM.

COVERING SHOULDER PADS

1 Cut a square of lining twice the length of the shoulder pad. Fold it in half diagonally and press in a crease.

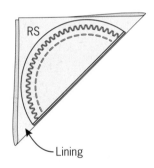

Lining

FIGURE 4 CUT AND FOLD A PIECE OF LINING TO COVER THE SHOULDER PAD.

2 Unfold the lining and place the shoulder pad centrally on the fabric with the straight edge on the fold. Refold the fabric, pinning and basting it around the shoulder pad.

3 Machine stitch around the curved edge of the pad. Then cut out the shape and neaten the edges

SLEEVE FINISHES

Sleeves can be finished with a simple double-turned and top-stitched hem, with self casing and elastic (see pp. 64–65) or with bias binding (see pp. 100–103). Fitted sleeves, however, need openings at the hem edge in order to get the sleeves on and off. These can then be finished with cuffs.

MAKING A SIMPLE SLEEVE OPENING

1 The simplest method is to stitch the underarm seam, stopping 3in (7.5cm) from the hem end. Neaten the seam allowances separately and press them open.

2 Top stitch the seam allowances in place around the opening. Add a cuff (see p. 110) or hem the sleeve and add a buttonhole and button.

RS

FIGURE 5 SIMPLY TOP STITCH THE SEAM ALLOWANCES AROUND THE OPENING.

MAKING A FACED OPENING

The steps below give the easiest method of attaching a separate placket, which produces a crisp neat finish.

1 Cut a 2 x 5 in (5 x 13cm) rectangle of fabric to make a facing. Neaten the long edges and one short edge.

2 With right sides together, place the facing on the sleeve end in the placket position (to the outer edge of the underwrist). Mark a dart ½in (1.3cm) wide at the lower end and 4in (5cm) long. Then stitch the facing to the sleeve following the marked line.

3 Cut up the centre of the dart, close to but not through the point of the dart.

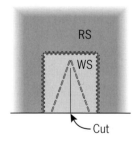

RS
WS
Cut

FIGURE 6 CUT UP THE DART, THROUGH THE FACING AND THE SLEEVE FABRIC.

4 Turn the facing to the inside and press. If desired, top stitch around the opening to keep the facing in place.

MAKING A CONTINUOUS LAP

This is a popular opening on a shirt sleeve, although it can be tricky to make if the lap fabric frays easily.

1 Create the opening in the sleeve by marking a narrow dart as in step 3, below left, for a faced opening. Stitch along the marked lines, reducing the stitch length 1in (2.5cm) on each side of the dart point. Then cut open the V-shape.

2 Cut a 7 x 1¼in (18 x 3cm) strip of fabric and neaten one long edge by turning and pressing it under.

3 With the cut edges of the garment spread wide so they almost form a straight line, pin the fabric strip to the cut raw edges and right sides together. With the garment uppermost, stitch the strip in place, stitching just to the left of the stay stitching and keeping the extra sleeve fabric out of the way. Press the seam allowance towards the lap.

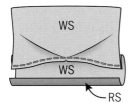

FIGURE 7 STITCH THE STRIP TO THE OPENED-OUT DART ON THE BOTTOM EDGE OF THE SLEEVE.

4 Fold the lap to the wrong side of the sleeve, encasing the raw edges, and slip stitch it in place. Finish by pressing the front of the lap to the inside of the sleeve. Stitch the underarm seam together.

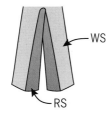

FIGURE 8 PRESS THE FRONT OF THE LAP TO THE WRONG SIDE OF THE SLEEVE.

CUFFS

Sleeves on shirts are generally finished with cuffs. These are made from a top, interfacing and under layer, although occasionally the top and under layer are cut as one and folded in half.

Turn-ups are another type of cuff that can feature on sleeves or trouser legs. They are formed by extending the sleeve or trouser leg hem edge, slightly shaping it at the fold line so that the extension can be neatened and turned back on itself.

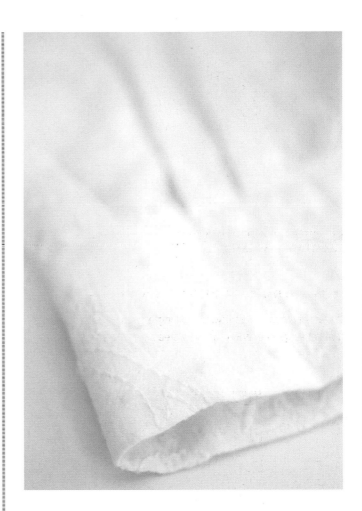

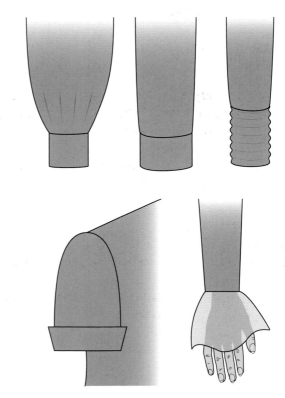

FIVE TYPES OF CUFF

MAKING SIMPLE CUFFS

1 Cut a rectangle of fabric that is the wrist circumference in length, plus 2in (5cm) for wearing ease and 1¼in (3cm) for seam allowances, and double the width required (6in (15cm) deep is a good average).

2 Apply interfacing to the wrong side of the cuff fabric.

3 With right sides together, fold the cuff in half widthways and sew the short ends together to form one continuous circle.

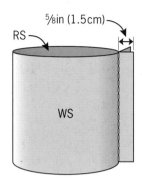

FIGURE 9 FOLD THE CUFF IN HALF WIDTHWAYS AND SEW THE SHORT ENDS TOGETHER.

4 Trim the seam allowances and then turn the cuff through to the right side. Neaten one long edge by turning under ⅝in (1.5cm) and pressing in place.

5 Attach the cuff to the sleeve end, right sides together, matching the raw edges and the cuff seam to the underarm seam.

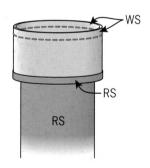

FIGURE 10 STITCH THE CUFF TO THE BOTTOM EDGE OF THE SLEEVE MAKING SURE YOU DON'T CATCH ANY OTHER PARTS IN THE STITCHING.

6 Press the seam allowances towards the cuff. Then fold the cuff down and slip stitch the neatened edge to the inside of the sleeve, encasing the raw edges.

MAKING CUFFS WITH OPENINGS

1 Cut out and interface the cuff, neatening one long edge as for a simple cuff (see steps 1–2, left).

2 Attach the cuff to the sleeve, with the opening on the sleeve in line with the seam line on each short end of the cuff. Stitch the cuff in place.

3 Fold the cuff in two, right sides together, so that the neatened edge will sit over the seam line. Sew the side edges in line with the sleeve opening edges.

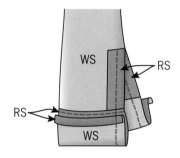

FIGURE 11 STITCH THE SIDE SEAMS ON THE ATTACHED CUFF IN LINE WITH THE EDGES OF THE SLEEVE OPENING.

4 Clip the seam allowances, cutting the corners at angles. Turn the cuff through, pushing the corners out with a point turner.

MAKING FLOUNCED CUFFS

A flounce gives a blouse a softer silhouette. It is usually cut from a circular or semi-circular piece of fabric, depending on the fullness actually required.

1 Cut the flounce with the inner curve the same as the circumference of the sleeve end, including 1¼in (3cm) for seam allowances. The width of the flounce will depend on personal preference, but about 4in (10cm) makes a nice deep flounce.

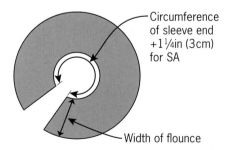

FIGURE 12 CUT ONE PIECE OF FABRIC FOR EACH FLOUNCE.

2 Join the straight ends, right sides together. Then hem the flounce with a narrow rolled hem (see p. 30) or by overlocking the edges.

3 Attach the flounce to the sleeve, right sides together, with the flounce join in line with the seam on the sleeve.

MAKING PLACKETS

A placket is a classic band on the sleeve or at the neck, and produces a smart traditional shirt finish when coupled with an opening cuff. It is created from a separate shaped and folded piece of fabric, and is attached to the sleeve end prior to stitching the underarm seam.

1 Commercial patterns will include a paper template for the placket; if making your own, follow the layout in Figure 13. Cut out the fabric and transfer all the markings.

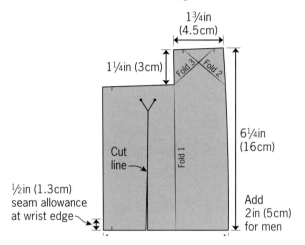

FIGURE 13 CUT OUT ONE PIECE OF FABRIC FOR EACH PLACKET, FOLLOWING THIS LAYOUT.

2 Place the placket on the sleeve, with the right side of the placket to the wrong side of the sleeve and the extension section towards the front of the sleeve.

3 Machine stitch along the stitching lines in a rectangle, starting and finishing at the lower edge. Cut up the centre of the box and into the corners, through both the placket and shirt fabrics.

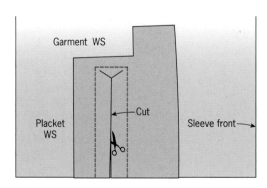

FIGURE 14 STITCH AROUND AND THEN CUT UP THE CENTRE OF THE BOX.

4 Turn the placket through to the right side of the sleeve and press the seam allowances towards the placket. Fold the short side edge of the placket under by ¼in (6mm) and press. Then place this folded edge on top of the stay stitching and pin and machine stitch it in place close to the edge.

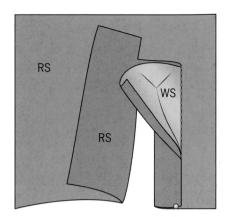

FIGURE 15 STITCH THE SHORT SIDE EDGE OF THE PLACKET.

5 Tuck the longer side edge of the placket under by ¼in (6mm) and press. Then fold the extension back so that the fold just covers the stitching line and the whole extension overlaps the shorter placket side.

6 Make a point at the top of the extension on the placket, by folding the corners over to make a point in the middle and pressing.

7 Machine stitch the long folded edges of the extension in position through just one side of the placket. Then stitch around the point of the placket through all the layers, as shown in Figure 16.

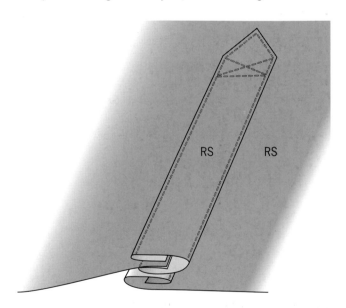

FIGURE 16 STITCH THE POINT OF THE PLACKET TO SECURE THE TOP END OF THE PLACKET TOGETHER.

COLLARS

Collars on shirts and blouses can be rolled, stand straight up or lie flat against the neck. A traditional tailored collar will also be attached to lapels and revers, front garment edges that are faced to turn back on themselves. Most collars have three layers: an upper and under collar and an interfacing.

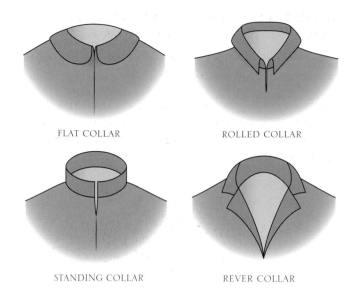

FLAT COLLAR   ROLLED COLLAR

STANDING COLLAR   REVER COLLAR

EXPERT TIP

Trim the under collar a tiny ¹⁄₁₆in (2mm) smaller than the upper collar so that the seam line will fall slightly on the underside.

MAKING ROLLED AND FLAT COLLARS

1 Cut the upper and under collars and the interfacing from the same pattern piece. Transfer any markings for the roll line, etc. to the fabric. Interface the upper collar section. If using fusible interfacing, cut off the seam allowances before fusing it to the reverse of the upper collar section.

EXPERT TIP

On jackets, also interface the lower collar section, with the interfacing cut on the bias.

2 Pin and baste the collar sections right sides together. Then stitch them together, starting at the centre back and working around to the front, reducing the stitch length 1in (2.5cm) on each side of the collar point. Repeat to the other side, leaving the neck edge open.

WS

FIGURE 17 STITCH THE LAYERS OF THE COLLAR TOGETHER AROUND THE OUTER EDGES.

3 Grade, clip and notch the seam allowances to minimize the bulk in the seams. Clip into the seam allowances, cutting points at an angle. Turn the collar through, pushing the corners out with a point turner and rolling the seam so that it just sits on the under collar side. Press from both sides.

4 Understitch the seam allowances to the under collar only as far as possible.

ATTACHING A COLLAR WITHOUT A FACING

1 Neaten the open edge of the upper collar by turning in a ¼in (6mm) seam allowance and pressing.

2 Stay stitch around the curved areas of the garment neckline. You many also need to clip into the seam allowance so the collar will match the neck edge smoothly.

3 With right sides together, pin the under collar section to the neckline of the garment, matching the notches, seam lines, etc. and keeping the upper collar section free. Stitch the collar in place and then grade, clip and notch the seam. Press.

4 Pin the neatened edge of the upper collar over the neckline seam and either slip stitch or stitch it in the ditch (see p. 25) from the right side.

ATTACHING A COLLAR WITH A FACING

1 Pin the collar to the garment through all layers and with the under collar closest to the right side of the garment. Clip the neck edge of the garment if necessary. Stitch the collar in place.

2 Neaten the outside edge of the facing. Then pin and stitch the facing over the collar, right sides together and matching raw edges.

3 Grade, clip and notch the seam allowances before turning the facing to the inside of the garment. Press the facing in place. Under stitch around the curved areas of the garment neckline.

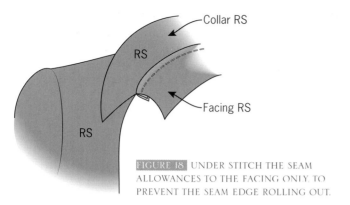

FIGURE 18 UNDER STITCH THE SEAM ALLOWANCES TO THE FACING ONLY, TO PREVENT THE SEAM EDGE ROLLING OUT.

MAKING STAND COLLARS

This type of collar stands straight up from the neck edge and include styles such as granddad collars and polo or turtle necks. It is often cut from a band of fabric on the straight grain.

1 Notch and clip the neck edge of the garment well in order to fit the collar.

2 Trim the seam allowance from the interfacing and fuse it in place on the collar so it sits just within the seam lines. Then turn under one long edge of the collar and press.

3 Pin and stitch the raw collar edge to the garment neck edge, right sides together and with just the seam allowance extending beyond the garment opening on one side and an overlap of 1in (2.5cm) on the other.

4 Fold the collar, right sides together, so the neatened long edge sits over the neck seam line. Finish the short ends by sewing from the fold to the seam line. On the overlapping end, pivot at the seam line and stitch towards the collar until the stitching meets the seam. Clip diagonally into the seam allowances where the stitching joins.

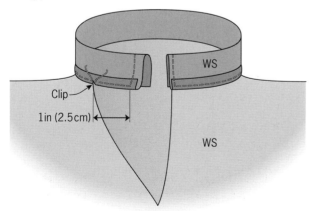

FIGURE 19 STITCH THE SHORT ENDS OF THE COLLAR RIGHT SIDES TOGETHER.

5 Then trim the seam allowances and press towards the collar. Turn the collar through to the right side and slip stitch or stitch it in the ditch to catch the neatened edge in place over the seam.

MAKING STRETCH KNIT STAND COLLARS

Use the quartering method to attach a stretch knit collar.

1 Join the short ends of the collar together to make a continuous circle. Then fold the collar in half lengthways, wrong sides together.

2 Divide the collar into four equal quarters. Divide the neck edge of the garment in the same way. Then pin both raw edges of the collar to the neck edge at the marked points, with right sides together and the collar seam at the centre back of the neck.

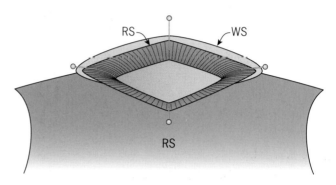

FIGURE 20 PIN THE COLLAR TO THE NECKLINE, MATCHING THE QUARTER POINTS.

3 Stretch the collar to fit as you machine stitch it in place.

MAKING TAILORED COLLARS

This type of collar is found on shirts and jackets. It consists of an upper collar and under collar with a stand. It is often attached to lapels or revers, which are sewn as part of the garment front. To add support and stability to tailored collars, you need to add extra layers of interfacing.

1 First interface the under collar as usual, but then interface the stand area between the roll line and the neck edge a second time.

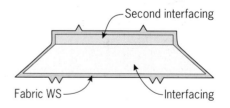

FIGURE 21 ADD AN EXTRA STRIP OF INTERFACING ACROSS THE COLLAR STAND.

2 To help the lapels roll out smoothly and evenly, fuse extra layers of interfacing between the roll line on the lapel and the edge. Cut the interfacing on the grain, with the grain running parallel to the roll line.

3 Once the garment is finished, use a seam roll (or a tightly rolled towel in a pillowcase) to press the rolled-over lapel in place.

STRAPS, TIES AND BONING

STRAPS AND TIES ARE IDEAL FOR PROVIDING A LITTLE MORE SUPPORT AND SECURITY, WHILE BONING GIVES THE ADDED BONUS OF MORE STRUCTURE FOR A CLOSER FITTING SILHOUETTE. STRAPS AND TIES CAN BE MADE FROM SELF-FABRIC, RIBBONS, BRAIDS OR CONTRASTING FABRIC. TO PREVENT UNWANTED STRETCH, CUT HALTER AND SHOULDER STRAPS ON THE STRAIGHT OF GRAIN, BUT CUT WAIST TIES ON THE BIAS TO PROVIDE FLEXIBILITY.

STRAPS

Anything over ½in (1.3cm) wide can be considered to be a strap. These are used to add support and also hide bra straps. They can have straight parallel edges or be shaped, even including gathering or pleating at the ends.

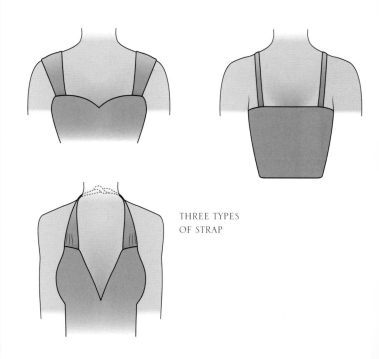

THREE TYPES OF STRAP

MAKING STRAPS

1 Cut the straps on the straight of grain. If using patterned fabric, make sure both straps are cut from the same part of the fabric design.

Boned top

Nothing shouts elegant evenings more than a beautiful boned top made in silk. This example is made in crinkle-finish raw silk. Encased boning has been stitched to the seam allowances down both long edges to prevent it from twisting. The bodice also features an open-ended zipper in the side seam so it is easy to get on and off.

❀ **The pattern is New Look 6480.**

2 Apply interfacing to the wrong side of the strap. Then fold it in half lengthways and sew the long seam. Trim the seam allowance and turn the strap through.

STITCH THE SEAM AND THEN TURN THE STRAP THROUGH.

3 Refold the strap so the seam is in at the centre of the underside and then press.

SEWING SENSE

It is easier to turn through two shorter parts than one long length. So, if making long straps, sew across one short end and part way along the long edge. Then leave a opening for turning in the centre of the long edge before continuing to stitch along that edge and across the second short one. Turn through and slip stitch the opening closed.

ADDING PLEATS

1 To add pleats at the strap ends, stitch the straps as in step 2 above, starting with a strip at least 6in (15cm) wide.

2 Turn the strap wrong side up so that the seam is in the centre. Then make a mark ½in (1.3cm) on each side of the seam line. Bring the marks to the centre seam, pin and stitch. This forms a box pleat on the right side of the strap.

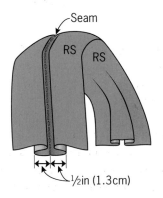

FORM A BOX PLEAT IN THE CENTRE OF THE STRAP.

MAKING SHAPED STRAPS

Straps that are wider at the shoulder and narrow at the bodice can be cut as two pieces, joined at the widest point or shoulder seam.

1 Cut two back and two front pieces for each shoulder strap from the shaped pattern piece.

2 Interface one front and one back piece. Then, with right sides together, join these two pieces at the shoulder seam. Press the seam open. Repeat for the other two pieces.

3 With right sides together, join the interfaced section to the plain section, leaving an opening for turning in one long edge just behind the shoulder seam.

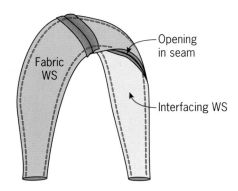

SEW THE TOP AND BOTTOM SECTIONS TOGETHER, LEAVING AN OPENING FOR TURNING.

4 Clip the seams and turn the strap through to the right side. Press the seam allowance on the opening to the inside. Slip stitch the opening closed.

TIES

There are two easy methods of making thin ties, which are narrower than straps. The first uses the cord method and the second a rouleau loop turner.

MAKING CORD-TURNED TIES

1 As for straps, cut the tie double the width plus seam allowances by the length required. Cut a length of cord, or string, at least 5in (13cm) longer.

2 Fold the fabric in half lengthways, right sides together, and place the cord within the fold so that a tail protrudes from the lower end. Machine stitch across one end, catching the cord in the stitching, pivot at the corner and stitch down the long length.

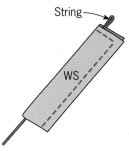

FIGURE 4 STITCH THE CORD INTO THE FABRIC AND THEN PULL ON IT TO TURN THE TIE THROUGH.

3 Neaten the seam allowances. Then pull on the cord to pull the tie through to the right side. Once completely through, cut off the cord and keep for repeat use.

MAKING ROULEAU LOOP TIES

Also known as spaghetti straps, these are very narrow ties.

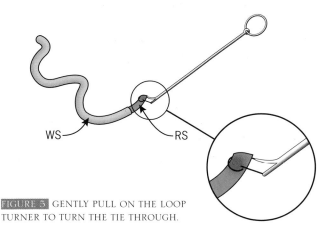

1 Cut the ties on the straight grain, twice the finished width required plus seam allowances. For a ⅜in (1cm) tie, this means a strip 1⅛in (3.5cm) wide. Sew the seams as usual.

2 Without cutting away the seam allowance, insert the rouleau loop turner into the tie. Hook the latch on the end over the fabric, piercing the weave and then gently pull on the loop turner to bring the tie through to the right side. The seam allowance will stuff the tie, giving it a nice rounded appearance.

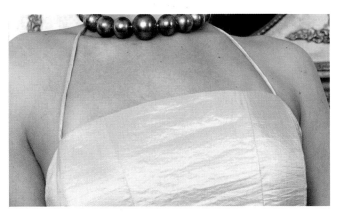

FIGURE 5 GENTLY PULL ON THE LOOP TURNER TO TURN THE TIE THROUGH.

ATTACHING STRAPS AND TIES

If a bodice is to be lined or have a facing, attach the straps or ties before applying the lining or facing.

1 With the raw edges matching, pin the strap to the right side of the garment front so that the seam on the strap is uppermost. Stitch the strap in place.

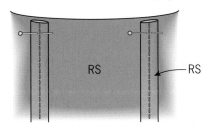

FIGURE 6 STITCH THE STRAPS TO THE BODICE FRONT, RIGHT SIDES TOGETHER.

2 Fold the seam allowances to the inside of the garment. Pin the strap in position on the back of the garment and try it on. Adjust the position of the strap as necessary. Mark the position on the strap and the garment, and take off the garment.

3 Repin the strap to the garment back, so the strap end hangs down, positioning the mark on the strap on the garment seam line. Stitch the strap in place and cut off any strap that extends beyond the seam line.

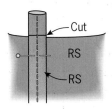

FIGURE 7 SEW THE STRAP TO THE BACK OF THE GARMENT, STITCHING FROM THE REVERSE OF THE STRAP.

4 Attach the facing or lining to the garment, right sides together and sandwiching the straps between the layers. When the garment is turned through to the right side, the straps will be uppermost and the right way up.

MAKING HALTER STRAPS

Attach the straps to the front of the garment as above. Then neaten the other short ends by tucking the raw edges inside the tube and slip or top stitching them in place. Knot the free ends together each time you wear the garment.

BONING

Boning adds structure and support to a bodice, making straps unnecessary. The more boning added, the greater the support given. It is usually attached to the seam allowances, keeping the garment in shape and preventing it from wrinkling with wear. Boning comes in many forms, from rigid encased nylon bought by the metre to flat metal and metal spirals cut to length and capped at each end.

EASY BONING

The easiest boning to use is the encased variety as you can attach it directly to seam allowances, stitching it down both long edges of the casing.

1 First interface and/or interline the main garment sections. Then stitch the seams and press the seam allowances open.

2 Centre the boning on the seam allowances, just within the seam lines at the top and bottom of the garment. Using a zipper foot, machine stitch down both long edges, stitching the boning casing to the seam allowances only or, making sure the thread matches the garment closely, stitch through all the layers so that there are two parallel rows of top stitching on each side of the seam on the right side of the garment.

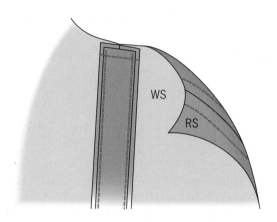

FIGURE 8 STITCH THE BONING TO THE WRONG SIDE OF THE MAIN BODICE.

EXPERT TIP

Boning naturally curves one way, so when you attach it, check the curve and make sure that it will work with the body shape.

MAKING CASINGS FROM SEAM ALLOWANCES

If the boning comes without casings, it would be best to make some, so that the garment is more comfortable to wear.

1 First interface the garment pieces as above and then stitch the seams, taking a regular seam allowance. Press the seam allowances to one side and neaten them together.

2 Stitch close to the neatened edge, stitching through all layers, including the main garment. Stitch across the top of the casing on the seam line.

3 Insert the boning into the casing from the bottom, between the garment and the seam allowance. Cut the end of the boning in a curve so there are no sharp edges or insert it into an end cap. To retain the boning in place, stitch across the bottom of the casing on the seam line.

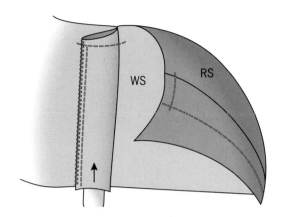

FIGURE 9 INSERT THE BONING INTO THE SEAM ALLOWANCE CASING.

APPLYING CASING TO OPEN SEAM ALLOWANCES

You can also make a casing to work with open seam allowances.

1 If working with seam allowances, stitch the seams as usual, neatening the raw edges separately. Then press the seams open.

2 Centre a length of ¾in- (2cm-) wide ribbon over the seam allowances. Pin and machine stitch the long edges to the seam allowance only. Stitch across the top of the casing along the seam line at the top of the garment. Insert the boning from the bottom.

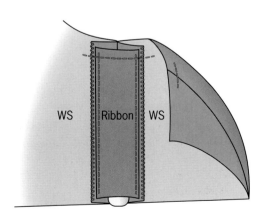

FIGURE 10 CREATE A BONING CASING WITH A LENGTH OF RIBBON.

APPLYING CASING TO A FABRIC SECTION

Sometimes it is advisable or necessary to add boning within a fabric section, for example, to the lower bodice to give more support to a fuller bust. This needs a dedicated casing.

1 Mark vertical placement lines equally spaced across the garment piece. Pin lengths of ribbon on the placement lines and stitch them in place along both long edges and across the top (the stitching will show on the right side of the garment).

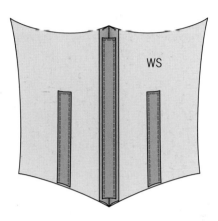

FIGURE 11 ATTACH RIBBON CASINGS OVER THE BONING PLACEMENT LINES.

2 Try the garment on and then cut the boning to the correct length, so that it will sit just within the bottom seam line.

SEWING SENSE
End caps for cut lengths of boning are available for most boning widths. They prevent the boning working its way through the fabric and/or digging into flesh. If not available, cut the boning into a neat curve at each end.

FABULOUS JACKETS

THE FINAL MUST-HAVE GARMENT FOR A CAPSULE WARDROBE IS A JACKET. THERE ARE MANY TYPES, FROM SUIT TO CASUAL OUTERWEAR, EDGE-TO-EDGE TO DOUBLE-BREASTED. EQUALLY DIVERSE IS THE TYPE OF FABRIC THAT CAN BE USED, WHICH DEPENDS ON STYLE AND THE ULTIMATE USE OF THE JACKET.

JACKETS DEFINITELY LOOK AND HANG BETTER IF THEY ARE LINED. NOT ONLY DOES A LINING GIVE MORE WEIGHT TO THE GARMENT, IT HIDES SEAMING AND MAKES IT EASIER TO SLIP THE JACKET ON AND OFF.

THIS CHAPTER SHOWS YOU JUST HOW SIMPLE IT IS TO USE MODERN INTERFACINGS TO ACHIEVE CRISP TAILORING, AS WELL AS HOW TO LINE VARIOUS GARMENTS AND ADD PROFESSIONAL DETAILS WITH BOUND BUTTONHOLES, WELT POCKETS AND PIPING.

TOP 10 JACKETS

CHOOSE YOUR JACKET TO SUIT YOUR LIFESTYLE. THIGH-LENGTH JACKETS ARE A GREAT COAT CHOICE IF YOU DRIVE A LOT. A COLLARLESS JACKET IS EASIER TO WEAR ALL DAY IN THE OFFICE AND A SOFT JACKET WORKS JUST AS WELL WITH JEANS AS IT DOES WITH A SMART SKIRT.

FITTED JACKET

This fitted style has princess seaming running from the shoulder or armhole to the waist at the back and front as well as a collar with revers and a front button closure. It's a smart style that can suit every figure shape. The length can vary, but ensure that the hemline doesn't fall on the widest part of the bottom or hips.

Fabrics: Tweeds, woollens, worsted, coatings, heavy raw silk and linen mixes

Special techniques: Speed tailoring, making buttonholes, adding collars and cuffs

Ease of sewing: Intermediate–advanced

CASUAL BELTED JACKET

Usually with a self-fabric tie belt, this style often has raglan sleeves, patch pockets and turn-up cuffs. Generally worn as a loose outer garment, it requires minimal fitting. Variations include cardigan-style wrap jackets.

Fabrics: Bouclés, woollens, wool mix

Special techniques: Adding patch pockets and turn-up cuffs, making buttonholes and tie belt

Ease of sewing: Easy–intermediate

BOXED, SEMI-FITTED JACKET

This is a classic suit-style jacket, typically teamed with a straight or pencil skirt or straight-legged trousers. It has a button front, can have a small collar or be collarless, and may have bust darts and/or princess seaming. The typical length is to the waist or just below.

Fabrics: Tweeds, woollens, bouclés for day wear; heavyweight silk, satin, brocade for evening wear

Special techniques: Making buttonholes, inserting darts

Ease of sewing: Easy–intermediate

JACKET WITH SHAWL COLLAR

On this more casual style of jacket, the shawl collar is made from the facing that turns out to the right side. This style is ideal for a double-sided fabric. It can be loose or semi-fitted and have shaping in the form of darts or princess seaming. The sleeves are often simpler raglan or drop-shoulder styles.

Fabrics: Fleece, felted wool, double-sided fabrics, faux fur

Special techniques: Working with double-sided fabrics or faux fur

Ease of sewing: Easy–intermediate

PEPLUM JACKET

This is an attractive waist-defining semi-fitted style. The peplum is a fuller 'skirt', attached to a waist seam or incorporated into front banding. Avoid this style if pear shaped as it will emphasis larger hips.

Fabrics: Woollens, wool mix, fleece for day wear; brocade, cottons, satins for evening

Special techniques: Making buttonholes, adding bias-cut peplum

Ease of sewing: Easy–intermediate

HOODED TOP

A very casual, sports-style jacket, this design will generally have an open-ended front zipper. Style variations include a front pouch pocket or side-seam pockets, a draw-string at the neck edge, and elasticated hem and sleeves.

Fabrics: Sweatshirting, double-knit jersey, fleece

Special techniques: Inserting open-ended zipper, elasticating a hemline, attaching patch pockets

Ease of sewing: Easy–intermediate

DOUBLE-BREASTED JACKET

Fitted or semi-fitted, this style suits small-busted silhouettes. It is a jacket design that can suit most occasions, depending on the length and fabric used – from suit jackets for the office in medium-weight wools to outerwear, thigh-length jackets in heavyweight fabrics.

Fabrics: Tweeds, woollens, fleece, gabardine, worsted, flannel

Special techniques: Making buttonholes, adding pockets, working with heavyweight fabrics

Ease of sewing: Intermediate–advanced

GILET

This is a sleeveless bodywarmer that can have an open-ended zipper or edge-to-edge closure. It may have inseam pockets, shaping with princess seaming and mandarin collar. It is usually padded for added warmth.

Fabrics: Fleece, faux suede, faux fur, double-sided fabric, polyester quilting fabric

Special techniques: Inserting open-ended zipper and pockets

Ease of sewing: Easy–intermediate

EDGE-TO-EDGE JACKET

This is a more casual style of jacket that can be dressed up or down for office or casual wear. In a boxy shape, it is also a regular feature in evening wear ensembles. The front edges meet at the centre and are either left unfastened or may have a single frog or hook and eye fastening. Usually collarless, some designs may have a shawl collar.

Fabrics: Felted woollens, tweeds, fleece for day wear; raw silks, satins for evening wear

Special techniques: Attaching decorative bias binding, inserting darts

Ease of sewing: Easy–intermediate

JACKET WITH ASYMMETRIC CLOSURE

This design detail can be used on a fitted or semi-fitted jacket. Often the closure style is emphasized with a contrast band or top stitching. The jacket can be any length from boxy waist-skimming to knee length.

Fabrics: Woollens, felted wool, bouclés for day wear; brocades, satins for evening wear

Special techniques: Adding contrast banding, making buttonholes

Ease of sewing: Intermediate–advanced

SPEED TAILORING AND DESIGNER TECHNIQUES

SPEED TAILORING IS THE TERM USED TO DESCRIBE A QUICK METHOD OF TAILORING THAT EVEN A NOVICE SEWER CAN TACKLE WITH CONFIDENCE, ARMED WITH A FEW BASIC TECHNIQUES. THIS CHAPTER ALSO COVERS SOME SPECIALIST TECHNIQUES SUCH AS BOUND BUTTONHOLES, WELT POCKETS AND PIPING — ALL OF WHICH ADD STYLISH DESIGNER DETAIL TO TAILORED JACKETS AND COATS.

TAILORING KIT

To make the process of tailoring easier, it's a good idea to have some special tools. In particular, a well-tailored garment needs to be well pressed and to do this, you need pressing aids. Using a pressing ham or sleeve roll combined with steam, you can press and shape fabrics more easily. For detail on the most suitable tools, see pp. 14–15.

SEWING SENSE

It is essential to use a good steam iron when tailoring. Fabric can be moulded and shaped with steam. Always allow the fabric to cool before handling it again.

Lined fitted jacket

Our thigh-length, fitted jacket has princess seaming, a shawl collar and a two-button closure above the high waistline. Here it is made in a wool blend and a seam roll has been added to the sleeve head to improve the line at the shoulders.

❀ **The pattern is Simplicity 2812.**

INTERFACINGS

The huge range of interfacings available today is what makes speed tailoring so accessible. Rather than adding layers of wadding, canvas and even horse hair, you can build up layers of different weights of interfacing in the areas that need extra support or body.

Woven interfacings are particularly useful for this process. Laid out and cut in the same manner as fabrics, following the grainline, they provide support and flexibility as and when it is needed. They come in different weights, to sew-in or fuse, and in different colours such as charcoal, black, white or nude. (See pp. 54–59 for more on interfacings.)

Some areas of a structured garment benefit from additional interfacing to reinforce them. These include lapel roll lines, revers, upper back panels, under collars with stands and hem edges.

INTERFACING LAPELS AND REVERS

1 Apply an additional layer of interfacing between the seam line and the roll line on the lapel or rever. Cut it from woven interfacing with the grainline running parallel to the roll line.

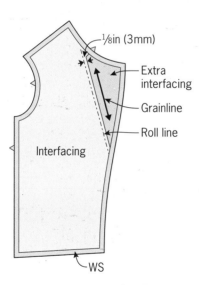

FIGURE 1 APPLY EXTRA INTERFACING FROM THE ROLL LINE TO THE SEAM LINE.

2 Fuse the interfacing a scant ⅛in (3mm) from the roll line to help the fabric fold over as it should. To press the rever in place, first put the garment front right side up on a flat surface. Then place a sleeve roll along the roll line, fold the lapel or rever back and steam it into shape by hovering the steam iron a few inches away and applying plenty of steam.

3 Allow the fabric to cool completely before continuing with the garment construction.

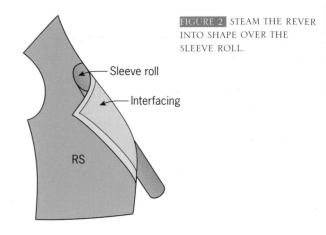

FIGURE 2 STEAM THE REVER INTO SHAPE OVER THE SLEEVE ROLL.

INTERFACING AN UNDER COLLAR

A smart shirt will have a stand collar, which has an upright section attached to the neck edge and an upper collar falling gracefully from the top of the stand. The stand is part of the under collar and if reinforced with extra interfacing, will hold its shape through repeated wear. (See p. 113 for how to apply interfacing to an under collar.)

INTERFACING AN UPPER BACK

Reinforcing the upper section of a jacket will aid the shape and provide a more structured finish. Simply add interfacing to the reverse of the upper back section, cutting the lower edge of the interfacing with pinking shears to avoid a definite ridge appearing on the right side of the fabric.

FIGURE 3 PINK THE BOTTOM EDGE OF THE INTERFACING TO PREVENT A RIDGE ON THE RIGHT SIDE.

INTERFACING HEM EDGES

Adding interfacing to the hem allowance ensures a well-structured hem.

1 First determine the required length of the garment. Then turn up the hem allowance and lightly press to form a crease. Neaten the raw edge as appropriate (see p. 23) and then unfold the hem allowance.

2 Cut a strip of interfacing to sit within the fold of the hem allowance and press it to the reverse of the garment just above the finished hemline.

3 When hemming, only stitch into the interfacing to ensure that no stitching is visible on the right side of the garment.

EXPERT TIP
To add more weight to a hem to prevent it flying about or riding up, add dress weights to the hem edges. These can be in the form of a chain laid in the foldline of the hem allowance or round button-like discs that are stitched to the edges and on the seam lines within the hem allowance.

UNDERLINING AND INTERLINING

As well as lining, a well-tailored garment may benefit from either underlining or interlining (but not usually both). Interlining adds warmth without bulk, while the extra layer of fabric of an underlining will add weight and stability to the fashion fabric as well as reducing its transparency.

1 Cut the interlining or underlining from the same pattern pieces as the main garment sections, excluding the facings, waistbands, collars and cuffs.

2 Transfer any pattern markings such as darts, folds or pleats to the right side of the underlining.

3 Pin the interlining/underlining pieces to the garment sections, wrong sides together and matching raw edges. Baste them in place approximately ½in (1.3cm) from the edges and through the darts, pleats and centre front line.

4 Once anchored securely together, treat each section as one layer and construct the garment according to the pattern instructions.

LININGS

All well-tailored jackets are lined. Lining fabric can be manmade polyester or a specialist lightweight silk called China silk or Jap silk. Sometimes it is advisable to use a more substantial fabric such as satin to line a special coat or jacket. Make sure the lining has the same laundry care as the main fabric.

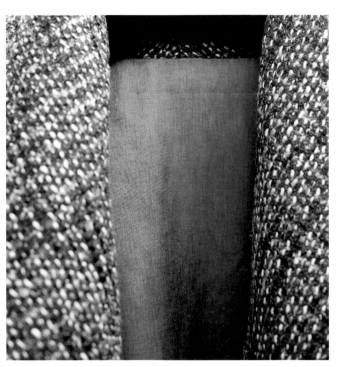

MAKING A LINING PATTERN

The aim of a lining is to add body, help the garment hang well and help to ease it on and off. As lining fabrics are tightly woven and have less flexibility than the garment fabric, the lining is usually cut slightly larger than the main garment to allow for movement and wearing ease at the centre back, bust and hems of the garment and sleeves. A commercial pattern will often have separate pattern pieces for the lining, but if not, make your own.

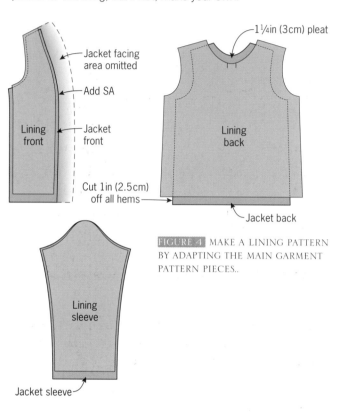

FIGURE 4 MAKE A LINING PATTERN BY ADAPTING THE MAIN GARMENT PATTERN PIECES..

1 Use the main garment pattern pieces (excluding the facings, collars and cuffs), but enlarge the tissue piece for the back section by adding approximately 1¼in (3cm) for a pleat from the neck to the hem at the centre back.

2 With the lining front pattern pieces on a flat surface, lay the facing pattern on top, matching the edges, and trace around the inner edge of the facing. Remove the facing and add a ⅝in (1.5cm) seam allowance outside the traced line and cut off the facing section.

3 Cut 1in (2.5cm) from the hem edges of all the lining pattern pieces.

INSERTING LININGS IN DRESSES, SKIRTS AND TROUSERS

1 Make up the lining in the same way as the main garment, with an opening in the zipper seam about 1in (2.5cm) longer than on the main garment. Neaten all the seam allowances and press.

2 Pin the lining to the garment, wrong sides together, by slipping the garment inside the lining and matching the neck or waist edges, side seams, darts and notches. For dresses, pin and stitch around the armholes and neckline. For skirts and trousers, stitch around the waist. On the zipper seam, turn the raw edge of the lining under and slip stitch it to the zipper tape by hand.

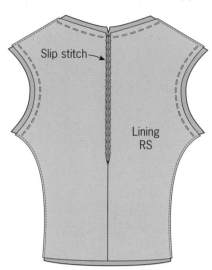

FIGURE 5 SLIP STITCH THE LINING TO THE ZIPPER TAPE.

SEWING SENSE

It is advisable to neaten the seam allowances of linings because, even though the seam allowances will be hidden between the garment and the lining, lining fabrics fray very easily.

3 Finish the armhole and neck edges with facings or bias binding so that, when they are turned to the inside, they will encase the raw edges of both the lining and the garment seam allowances.

4 Turn up the hem edges separately, turning the lining hem up more so that it sits just over the top of the garment hem allowance. (For hemming techniques, see p. 29–31).

INSERTING A LINING IN A JACKET

1 Make up the lining in the same way as the main garment, adding a pleat to the centre back neck edge, and excluding the facings, collars and cuffs. Neaten all the seam allowances and press as you go.

2 Sew the under collar to the main jacket neckline. Then sew the jacket facings together following the pattern instructions. Sew the facing to the upper collar section. With right sides together, sew the facing/upper collar to the lining at the sides and neckline, beginning and ending the seam 5in (13cm) from the hem edge.

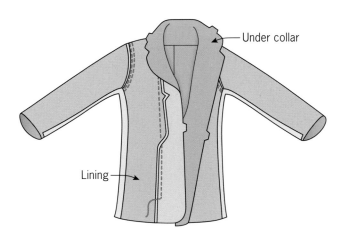

FIGURE 6 SEW THE JACKET FACINGS AND UPPER COLLAR SECTION TO THE LINING ALONG THE SIDE AND NECK EDGES.

3 Now pin, baste and machine the outer edges of the facings/ upper collar to the jacket body, with right sides together and matching all notches, seams, etc. Trim, grade, notch and clip the seam allowances. Press carefully and turn the garment right side out.

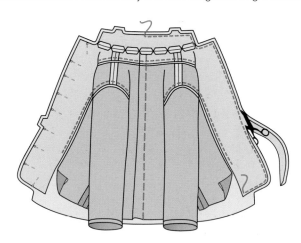

FIGURE 7 SEW THE OUTER EDGES OF THE FACINGS AND UPPER COLLAR TO THE JACKET.

4 Turn up the jacket hem, having interfaced the hem allowance (see left), and herringbone or blind hem stitch it in place.

5 Then turn up the lining hem allowance so that it is level with the jacket hem. To create the wearing ease, push the lining hem up about ¾in (2cm) and slip stitch the edge to the hem allowance of the jacket. Note that where the lining is attached to the facing, the hem edges will be level.

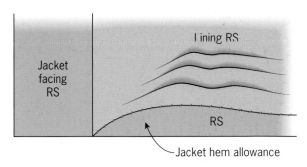

FIGURE 8 SLIP STITCH THE BOTTOM OF THE LINING HEM, PUSHING IT UP TO CREATE WEARING EASE.

BAGGING A LINING

This is a super fast way of attaching a lining to the main garment by machine.

1 Sew the jacket components together as usual. Do the same for the lining, but leave part of one side seam partially unstitched. Pin or hand baste the opening in the side seam.

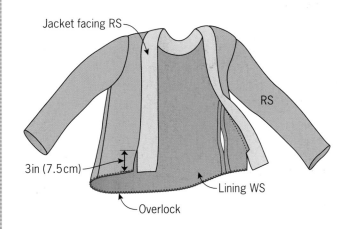

FIGURE 9 MAKE UP THE LINING BUT LEAVE ONE SIDE SEAM PARTIALLY UNSTITCHED.

2 Check that the main jacket hem length and sleeve lengths are accurate. Then temporarily hem the jacket and sleeves by turning up the hem allowance, hand basting ¼in (6mm) from the fold and lightly steaming the hem fold to form a crease to use as a stitching guideline later. On the jacket, undo the basting stitches for the width of the facings so that you can sew the lining to the facing.

3 Check that the lining and jacket are the same width by comparing the width of the lining at the hem with the width of the jacket, and matching the side seams, front edges and centre back seams if applicable. If the lining is too small, let out the seams a little; if too big, take them in a little. Failure to ensure a good fit can result in the jacket hem being pulled out of shape or the lining creasing unattractively.

4 As before, sew the inner edge of the jacket facing to the lining, with right sides together and in one continuous seam, starting and finishing 3in (7.5cm) from the hem on each side.

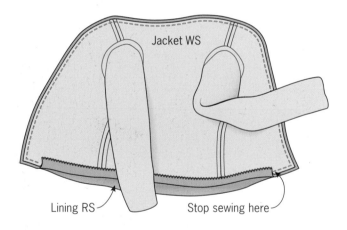

FIGURE 10 SEW THE JACKET TO THE LINING/FACING IN ONE CONTINUOUS SEAM.

5 Keeping right sides together, unfold the jacket hem allowance and pin the lining hem edge to the jacket hem edge, matching the side seams. Then machine stitch the hem edges together.

6 Turn the jacket right sides out through the opening in the lining side seam. Turn the jacket hem up at the crease made earlier and baste the hem in place to set it. The excess lining is called a jump hem, which allows for movement and ease.

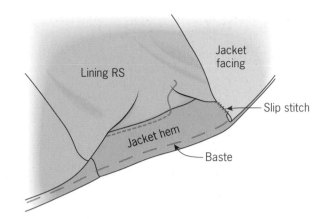

FIGURE 11 BASTE THE HEM IN PLACE CLOSE TO THE FOLD AND AT THE TOP OF THE HEM ALLOWANCE.

7 To machine stitch the sleeve lining to the jacket sleeve, again make sure the widths of both are the same. Then with the jacket right sides out, pull the lining down the sleeve, wrong sides together. Unfold the sleeve hem allowance and pin the seams together with one pin at the seams.

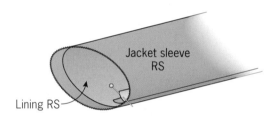

FIGURE 12 WITH THE JACKET SLEEVE HEM ALLOWANCE UNFOLDED, PIN THE LINING TO THE SLEEVE AT THE SEAMS.

8 Pull the sleeve out through the opening in the lining side seam so that the sleeve is wrong side out. Pull the jacket sleeve from the lining sleeve so they face each other, joined by the one pin at the side seam. Remove the pin and roll the lining so that the wrong side is out. Line up the raw edges of the hems and stitch them together close to the neatened edges.

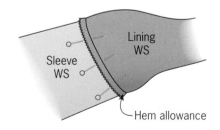

FIGURE 13 STITCH THE LINING AND JACKET SLEEVE HEMS TOGETHER.

9 Turn the sleeve right side out through the opening in the jacket lining side seam. Push the lining back up into the sleeve and, if desired, catch the excess at the side seam. Attach the lining to the other sleeve in the same way.

ALTHOUGH THIS BOLERO WAS FINISHED WITH BIAS BINDING, INSTEAD THE FABRIC AND LINING COULD
HAVE BEEN BAGGED AND THEN A TRIM APPLIED AROUND THE EDGES OF THE FINISHED GARMENT.

BOUND BUTTONHOLES

Bound buttonholes are usually a regular rectangle shape and made from self-fabric to match the garment. However, they can be in contrast fabric and even a variety of shapes to create a design feature.

MAKING A BOUND BUTTONHOLE

1 First determine the buttonhole position and measure the button diameter. Mark the diameter measurement with a chalk line on the buttonhole placement, adding ⅛in (3mm) to the length.

2 Fuse some interfacing to the reverse of the fabric behind the buttonhole placement to help prevent the fabric stretching or fraying as it is handled.

3 Cut a strip of the main or contrast fabric 1in (2.5cm) longer than the buttonhole by 2in (5cm) wide and interface it to stabilize it. On the reverse of this strip, mark the buttonhole length to match that on the garment.

4 Then pin the strip, right sides together, over the buttonhole placement, matching the chalk lines.

5 Stitch a rectangle around the chalk line, ⅛in (3mm) above and below the line. Carefully snip into and cut along the chalk line, clipping diagonally into the corners close to, but not through, the stitching.

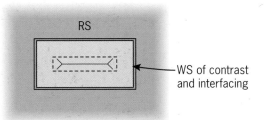

FIGURE 14 CUT ACROSS THE HOLE AND INTO THE CORNERS.

6 Pull the strip through to the wrong side. Press the little cut lip on one long edge towards the buttonhole. Fold the buttonhole fabric over the lip so that it fills half the hole. Repeat for the other long edge, so that the folded edges meet along the centre of the buttonhole. Carefully turn the garment to the right side and press the buttonhole fabric. Hand baste the buttonhole edges (welts) together.

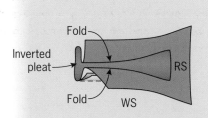

FIGURE 15 PULL THE PATCH THROUGH AND REFOLD BOTH LONG EDGES TO CLOSE ALONG THE CENTRE OF THE BUTTONHOLE.

7 Turn back to the wrong side and hand stitch the side edges of the buttonhole fabric in place where small inverted pleats are formed by the folded fabric. Then working from the right side, stitch in the ditch (see p. 25) along the edges of the welts.

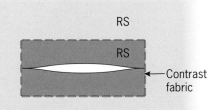

FIGURE 16 HAND STITCH THE WELTS IN PLACE.

WELT AND JETTED POCKETS

The welts of these pockets are formed in a similar way to bound buttonholes, with the addition of a pocket bag. A breast pocket will have one welt, while back pockets may be jetted, with an upper and a lower welt.

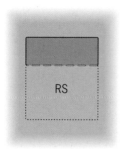

WELTED BREAST POCKET

WELTED BACK POCKET

MAKING A POCKET WITH ONE WELT

1 Cut a piece of fabric to make the welt; it should be at least 1in (2.5cm) longer than the pocket width and about 3in (7.5cm) deep. Interface the welt and also the reverse of the main fabric where the pocket is to be placed.

2 Draw the pocket placement lines, or transfer them from the commercial pattern, on the right side of the garment section using a chalk pencil.

3 Fold the welt fabric in half, right sides together. Stitch the short sides together, trim the seams, turn through and press. Pin and baste the long edges of the welt together.

4 Position the welt on the pocket placement line, so that the seam line on the welt is in line with the bottom stitching line of the pocket. Stitch the welt in place and trim the seam allowance of the welt to a scant ⅛in (3mm).

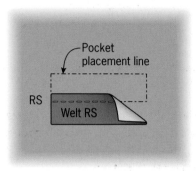

FIGURE 17 STITCH THE WELT TO THE LOWER PLACEMENT LINE.

5 Now prepare the pocket bag by cutting a rectangle twice the pocket length and the same width as the welt section. Mark the pocket placement lines in the centre of the pocket bag. With right sides together, place the pocket over the garment, matching the pocket placement lines and sandwiching the welt between the two. Pin the pocket section in place so that half is above the welt and half below.

6 Starting in the centre of the upper pocket placement line, stitch towards but stop just short of the first corner, take one stitch at an angle to the vertical side, then count the number of stitches as you stitch down the side to the bottom stitching line (to which the welt is stitched). Pivot and stitch along the bottom line through all thicknesses to the next corner. Pivot and count the stitches as you sew up to the top line to ensure that both sides are exactly the same. Again stitch one stitch at an angle and then continue along the top line to meet the start.

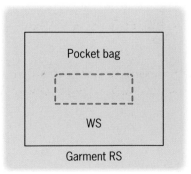

FIGURE 18 STITCH THE BAG AROUND THE PLACEMENT LINES.

7 Cut along the centre of the pocket placement stitching, cutting through the pocket bag and the garment, and clipping diagonally into the corners, close to but not through the stitching (as for a bound buttonhole, Figure 14, p. 130). Push the bag and welt through the opening so that the welt folds up to cover the hole. Press.

8 From the wrong side, fold the pocket bag in half so the sides and ends are even and then stitch, keeping the garment out of the way.

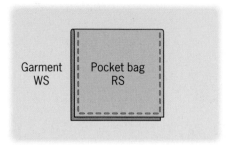

FIGURE 19 STITCH THE SIDES AND END OF THE POCKET BAG.

9 Finish by hand stitching the short ends of the welt in place on the right side of the garment.

EXPERT TIP

For a jetted or double welt pocket, add the second welt to the upper stitching line in the same manner as the lower welt, before attaching the pocket bag.

PIPING

Another stylish technique often used on designer wear and tailored garments is piping. This is added to seams to give definition, provide a contrast or highlight a particular design feature. Piping can be made from ready-made flanged piping, self fabric or contrast fabric.

PIPING ALONG PRINCESS SEAMS

MAKING FABRIC PIPING

1 Cut fabric strips on the bias (see p. 100) at least 1–1½in (2.5–3.5cm) wide. Join strips together to give the required length.

2 Fold the fabric in half lengthways, wrong sides together, sandwiching the piping cord within the fold. Pin or baste the long edges together.

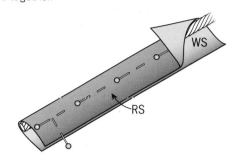

FIGURE 20 PIN OR BASTE THE PIPING CORD INSIDE THE FABRIC.

ATTACHING PIPING

1 Pin the piping to the right side of one main garment piece, matching the raw edges of the garment and the piping tape. Using a zipper foot, stitch the piping in place to the seam allowance close to the seam line.

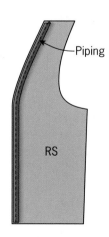

FIGURE 21 STITCH THE PIPING IN PLACE USING A ZIPPER FOOT.

2 Add the second garment piece, right sides together, sandwiching the piping between the layers of fabric. With the piped section uppermost, machine stitch the seam, sewing to the left of the previous stitching, closer to the piping tape.

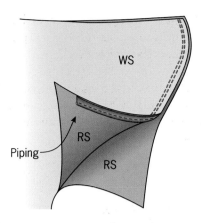

FIGURE 22 STITCH THE TWO GARMENT SECTIONS TOGETHER WITH THE PIPING BETWEEN.

3 Trim, clip and notch the seam allowance. Turn through to the right side so that the piping is on the edge of the seam.

JOINING PIPING ENDS

Occasionally it may be necessary to join two ends of piping. This is the neatest way.

1 First turn one short end of the piping fabric over to the wrong side by ¼in (6mm). Starting with that end, pin the piping to the garment section as above.

2 When the ends meet, overlap the end over the beginning by 1in (2.5cm). With the piping fabric open, trim the cord so that the ends meet exactly and hand stitch them together to secure them in place.

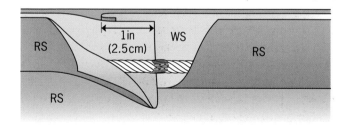

FIGURE 23 TRIM THE UPPER LAYER OF FABRIC AND CORD TO MAKE A NEAT JOIN.

3 Replace the fabric, folding it back over the cord, and continue to stitch it in place. Add the second garment section as above.

TROUBLESHOOTING TIPS

You can breath a huge sigh of relief because it's true – nobody is perfect! Things do go wrong, even for those who have been sewing for many years. Here is a guide to avoiding problems in the first place, and then a list of the most common problems with some helpful solutions.

AVOIDING PROBLEMS

This quick-check eight-step guide will help you avoid many potential problems.

1 Keep the bobbin race clean. Remove the bobbin after every sewing session and brush out the bobbin case. Occasionally, remove the bobbin casing (check how to do that in your user manual) and brush out underneath. You can also use a small vacuum cleaner to suck out the fluff and dust. Fluff can prevent the bobbin working properly, prevent the needle thread linking up with the bobbin thread, and more.

2 Use the right size and kind of needle for the fabric and thread, and replace the needle regularly.

EXPERT TIP

If you use a needle for a short burst of sewing and may use it again, paint the shank with nail polish to colour code it. Then you can easily find it again.

3 Choose good quality threads to suit your project – cottons with cotton fabric, polyester or polyester-covered cottons for manmade fabrics, silk for silk, etc. Avoid cheap threads, as they tend to break easily, and old threads, as they may have weakened over time.

4 When threading the machine, raise the presser foot to ensure the tension discs are released so the thread will slip easily through the thread path.

5 Use a thread retainer to hold the thread reel in place on the spindle, especially if the spindle lies horizontally. This will prevent it bouncing up and down as you sew or the thread getting tangled around the spindle, which can cause the thread to flow unevenly, uneven stitches, the thread to get tangled or break, or the needle to break.

6 Raise the needle when changing the stitch pattern as it may move from side to side through the stitch selection, possibly hitting the throat plate and bobbin mechanism, which may cause it to bend or break. Then try out the full new stitch pattern by turning the balance wheel towards you by hand to ensure the needle doesn't hit the side of the foot or throat plate. If it does, check the correct foot is being used and that the needle is not bent.

7 Test any stitch on scraps of the same fabric, using the same number of layers and interfacings.

8 Many modern machines are self-lubricating and so do not need oiling. However, check your user manual and oil as indicated, if required. Do get your machine serviced regularly – even if it is self-lubricating, it needs an overhaul occasionally!

SKIPPED OR BROKEN STITCHING

Broken or skipped stitches can be caused for a number of reasons, from incorrect or blunt needles, to thread getting caught on the spindle or not going through the tension discs properly. Try the remedies below:

SEWING SENSE

Always make sure the presser foot is raised and the needle is in the highest position when threading the sewing machine. Failure to do so can mean the thread doesn't go through the tension discs properly.

1 Rethread the top thread, making sure the presser foot is raised.

2 Ensure the thread is coming off the reel the right way (from underneath the reel or up and over; refer to your user manual).

3 Remove the bobbin and, using the little brush supplied with your machine, clean any fluff out of the bobbin race.

4 Make sure the bobbin is inserted the right way up so the thread comes off it and through the bobbin tension the right way (refer to the diagram on the bobbin cover or throat plate).

5 Check the needle is the right type for the fabric. For example, failure to use a ballpoint needle with stretch fabrics can cause skipped stitches.

6 Check the needle is the right size for the fabric and thread. A needle that is too large or heavyweight can cause skipped stitches on lightweight fabric, whereas a needle that is too small can break or make the seam pucker. (See the needle size chart on p. 12.) Thread may also break if the needle eye is too small. Try a larger eyed needle (for example, a jeans or an embroidery needle) or, for metallic threads, use a metalfil needle with a coated eye.

SEWING SENSE
If working with several layers, try a heavier needle than you would normally use for that type of fabric.

7 Check the condition of the needle. A blunt needle, or one with a virtually invisible burr in the eye, can shred or break the thread as it travels through at speed.

8 On stretch fabrics, stitch seams that need to stretch with a zigzag or stretch stitch.

TOP THREAD CLEARLY VISIBLE ON UNDERSIDE OR BOBBIN THREAD ON THE TOP

This is another problem that can be caused by incorrect threading. A perfectly formed stitch has the top thread on the top of the fabric, and the bobbin thread on the underside, intertwined between the fabric layers. To try to resolve the problem, take these steps:

1 Before adjusting the tension, rethread both bobbin and top threads to make sure they are correctly threaded and the bobbin is the right way up.

2 Make sure the stitch length, and the width if applicable, is suitable for the weight of fabric and number of layers being stitched. Lightweight fabrics can be stitched with a short stitch of 2–2.2, while fleece or layers of denim may need a 3.5 stitch length.

3 If steps 1 and 2 don't help, alter the top tension slightly, turning the dial to a higher number to tighten it and to a lower number to loosen it.

SEWING SENSE
It is rarely necessary to alter tensions on modern machines and a small alteration to tighten or loosen the tension goes a long way, so adjust very slowly, a little at a time.

TROUBLESOME NEEDLES

Problems can also occur if a needle isn't inserted properly, is blunt or damaged, or is the wrong type. It's very important to change needles regularly – every eight hours of sewing or every garment. Blunt needles are bad news!

NEEDLE BREAKS

1 Needles often break or bend when they hit or rub against the presser foot or the throat plate. Check that the needle clears both by turning the balance/fly wheel towards you by hand. Replace a broken or bent needle.

2 Check the needle is properly and fully inserted (usually with the flat side to the back, but check your user manual). Tighten the retaining screw by hand initially and then finish tightening with the screwdriver supplied in the tool kit. Failure to tighten the screw sufficiently may result in it working loose as the machine stitches, which will allow the needle to wobble, bend and break.

3 Make sure you use the right size of needle (see step 6, left).

4 Keep the thread reel in place with a thread retainer (see step 5, p. 134).

5 When stitching very dense designs or over another part of a stitch design, use a new machine embroidery needle which has a larger eye and can cope with dense stitching. Also use machine embroidery thread, which is lighter and finer, and so suited to densely stitched patterns.

NEEDLE STICKS

If a needle appears to be sticky or sticks as it goes up and down, it may have craft glue or remnants of glue from fusible interfacings on it. Use a cleaning agent, white vinegar or alcohol to clean it. Dry it thoroughly before reinserting it.

NEEDLE LEAVES HOLES

If there are holes right next to the stitches, the needle might be blunt or too large for the fabric. Replace it with a needle that is suitable for the fabric being stitched.

TYPES OF FABRIC

ACETATE – a chemically made fibre that can be added to other fabrics to give a silky finish; a great background fabric for machine embroidery, it can be disolved with acetone to give a lace-like finish

ACRYLIC – another synthetic fibre that is often added to other fibres to give warmth to the fabric

ALPACA, ANGORA – both are luxury wool fibres; alpaca comes from the llama; Angora is woven from angora goat hair; they both produce a soft, silky fabric, but Angora is often woven with other fibres to make a woollen cloth for coating

BARATHEA – a traditional woollen fabric, orginally made from silk/wool mixture, it is very smooth with a broken rib pattern

BOUCLÉ – term used to describe a thick, stubbly surface texture; bouclés can be knitted or woven and usually have a dull textural surface; ideal for jackets, waistcoats, etc.

BROADCLOTH – traditionally made of cotton, it is a light, tightly woven fabric with a soft, slightly napped surface

BROCADE – a luxurious heavyweight fabric that usually incorporates a jacquard design of flowers and leaves; used for evening wear

BROIDERIE ANGLAIS (EYELET EMBROIDERY) – traditionally a cotton fabric, it has self-coloured embroidered holes as a decorative finish

BUCKSKIN – an inexpensive leather from deer or elk skin

CALICO (MUSLIN IN USA) – an inexpensive cotton fabric, plainly woven with a smooth finish; different weights are available; often used to make a toile (a sample garment for checking the fit)

CAMEL HAIR – a luxury fibre woven from the under hair of a camel, it is usually mixed with sheeps' wool to combine luxury with durability; it is usually left undyed and has a soft yellow colour

CASHMERE, MELTON AND MOHAIR – made into luxury fabrics; use the 'with nap' layouts; test press a scrap first to check whether it flattens the pile; trim the pile from, or grade, seam allowances or use lining for facings to reduce bulk

CHAMBRAY – traditionally cotton, with the warp woven in white; similar in appearance to denim but lighter

CHEESECLOTH – a loosely woven cotton fabric, used for crafts or as lightweight fashion items

CHENILLE – a pile yarn with a knitted or woven finish that has a fuzzy or novelty texture

CHIFFON – a sheer, light drapeable fabric originally made of pure silk; used for wraps, as over-blouses or skirts

CHINA/JAP SILK – usually used as lining, it is lightweight with a plain weave

CIRÉ – a lightweight fabric with extremely slippery, shiny finish

CORDUROY – traditionally made in cotton, it is a corded fabric with a woven or sheared rib with a velvet-like nap

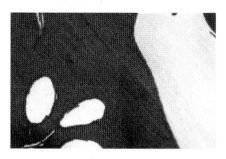

COTTON, POLYESTER/COTTON – lightweight, suitable for summer clothing; easy to sew and launder; available in a huge variety of colours and designs

COTTON BATISTE – a very lightweight soft, sheer fabric; can also be made in wool or synthetic fibres

COTTON KNITS – usually a fine gauge fabric, cotton knits are extensively used in fashion and sportswear; often mixed with other fibres for greater durability and less shrinkage

COTTON LAWN – crisp, lightweight cotton often used for heirloom stitching, christening gowns or lining for bridal wear

CREPE, CHALLIS – lightweight fabrics woven with a crepe yarn that creates a crinkled surface; easy to sew, minimum stretch along grain lines; fusible or sew-in interfacing is suitable

CREPE-BACKED SATIN (SATIN-BACKED CREPE) – double-sided fabric often used for bridal and evening wear

CREPE DE CHINE – traditionally a pure silk, lightweight fabric; modern manmade fibres make it more versatile and hardwearing

DENIM – a medium to heavyweight and hard-wearing twill weave fabric; the coloured warp and white weft is a very distinctive combination; traditionally blue but now in a range of colours

DOBBY/PIQUÉ – has a small pattern in the weave, similar to but less elaborate than a jacquard

DOUBLE KNIT – this is a firm knitted fabric that is very stable; looks the same on both sides and has a fine lengthwise rib

DRILL, CANVAS – heavier weight cottons for outdoor or hardwearing items; drill has a strong twill weave; canvas is also used for interfacings

DUPION – woven from two fibres of silk together, has a thick, uneven texture; makes lovely tops and lightweight jackets; synthetic dupion is less expensive

FAILLE – traditionally made of silk or cotton, it has a narrow crosswise rib which gives it a slightly heavier finish than crepe de chine

FIBRE – the plant or synthetic substance from which a fabric is woven

FLANNEL – has a soft, brushed appearance and is often used for pants or suits

FLANNELETTE – a lightweight fabric, usually made from cotton and used for children's nightwear

FLEECE – a fabulous fabric that is easy to work with, comes in many colours and designs, doesn't need neatening, washes easily and can be used for many outerwear garments; press with care as hot irons leave marks; use a slightly larger than usual seam allowance to help feed fabric layers evenly; trim close to stitching to reduce bulk in seams

FUR, FAKE/FAUX FUR – can have a long shaggy pile or be close cut; fake furs do not need neatening; trim fur pile from seam allowances to reduce bulk; cover seams using a sturdy pin to pick out the fur along the right side of seams

GABARDINE – a strong fabric with a close twill weave, ideal for suits, jackets, pants or lightweight coats

GAUZE – a very lightweight sheer fabric, usually made of cotton or silk

GEORGETTE – sheer; made with crepe yarns for a slightly more opaque finish than chiffon

GINGHAM – a crisp, cotton fabric with a two-tone check

HERRINGBONE – traditionally made in wool, it has a twill weave, reversed to create the effect of a herring backbone; used mainly for coatings and suitings

JERSEY – originally this was a knit fabric with purl stitches on the right side and plain stitches on the reverse; can now include other soft, lightweight knitted fabrics

LAMÉ, LYCRA®, SPANDEX – speciality fabrics used for exotic, dance or swimwear; lamé has a mixture of metallic yarns and can be woven or knitted, Lycra® is a two-way stretch fabric that is tightly woven and comes in many colours

LINEN, HANDKERCHIEF LINEN, LINEN-LIKE – linens feature creases; treat them as cottons; handkerchief linen is very lightweight

LODEN – a thick, heavy, napped fabric, similar to duffel cloth, used for coats

MELTON – a densely woven fabric with a slight nap and very smooth appearance, used for coats and uniforms.

MOHAIR – made from the angora goat; used alone or mixed with other fibres for suitings and coatings

MUSLIN – a plain weave fabric that is usually lightweight and used for interfacings

NUN'S VEILING – a plain weave, sheer fabric

NYLON – a man-made fibre that adds toughness and durability to other fabrics

ORGANDIE, ORGANZA – a lightweight sheer, fabric, slightly crisper than chiffon; organdie is traditionally made from cotton, organza from silk

OTTOMAN – has a crosswise rib, slightly wider than faille; traditionally made in wool

PEAU DE SOIE – traditionally made from pure silk, now also made in polyester; has a soft lustre and is slightly heavy in weight; ideal for evening wear and bridal gowns; polyester version is often known as peau

POLYESTER, VISCOSE, RAYON, POLYESTER CREPE DE CHINE – man-made fabrics that mimic the handle and look of natural fibres but are often cheaper to buy and easier to sew; will ravel easily so needs to be neatened well

POPLIN – woven with a fine horizontal rib, it is slightly heavier and crisper than cotton lawn

SAIL CLOTH – a very firmly woven cotton canvas used for sails

SATEEN – a strong, lustrous fabric usually made from cotton; different to satin

SATIN, SATIN-BACKED CREPE, DUCHESSE SATIN – a high sheen fabric; use 'with nap' layout to ensure even shading; satin is medium weight and ideal for evening wear; satin-back crepe is double-sided and ideal for evening suits; duchesse satin has a highly lustrous sheen on one side and is used in bridal wear

SEERSUCKER – has a permanently puckered or crinkled effect in alternating stripes

SERGE – has a twill weave; a traditional hardwearing suiting fabric

SHANTUNG – traditionally a plain weave silk fabric with occasional slubs

SILK NOIL, RAW SILK – have a raw or nubbed surface texture and shading; treat as pile fabric and use 'with nap' layout

STRETCH VELOUR – has a tightly woven short cut pile, similar to velvet; used for leisure and sportswear

SYNTHETIC LEATHER/ SUEDE – include faux suede, ultra suede, suedette, leatherette, leather

TAFFETA, PAPER TAFFETA, MOIRÉ TAFFETA – originally a plain weave silk fabric, it has a crisp finish and shiny surface; paper taffeta is lightweight and very crisp; moiré has a watermark finish and is usually luxurious and crisp

THAI SILK – silk from Thailand, heavily slubbed and often brightly coloured or iridescent

TULLE – traditionally a fine silk net used for bridal veils

TWEED: HARRIS, IRISH, SCOTTISH, DONEGAL – named after their origins; traditionally woven from wool with coloured slubs of yarn giving it a shaded, textured surface that may be slightly hairy; normally heavyweight and may have a nap and directional weave, so use 'with nap' layout

TWILL – a type of weave with slightly raised pattern; the weft thread weaves under and over pairs of warp threads

VELVET: PANNE, VELVETEEN, SCULPTURED AND DEVORÉ – luxury pile fabrics that can be manmade, cotton or silk, floaty and lightweight or heavyweight; devoré has parts of the pile burned away to leave a pattern; use 'with nap' layout

VICUNA – one of the most expensive and luxurious of wools, it is woven from llama hair; hard to dye, so usually natural colour of brown

VOILE – a very lightweight, sheer fabric with plain weave; can be used for summer wraps

WORSTED – term used to describe the way yarns are carded and combed to eliminate short fibres, thus producing a smooth surface (woollens are just carded and not so durable)

GLOSSARY

A-line – skirt that is angled outwards from the waist to the hem, like an A

Appliqué – additional fabric or motif attached to the surface of the base cloth; usually stitched in place with satin stitch

Back stitch – hand or machine (reverse stitch) used to anchor the stitches at the start and finish of a seam

Bagging – a method of attaching lining to the garment by sewing machine; they are stitched, right sides together, and then turned through at the hem edge

Ballpoint needle – needles with a slightly rounded tip; used for jersey and stretch fabrics; the tip parts the fibres rather than pierces them

Basting (tacking) – temporary stitching to hold layers of fabric together

Batting (wadding) – a soft fleecy layer of fused fibres, used to add bulk and warmth

Bias – the stretchiest part of the fabric, at 45-degree angle from the selvage

Bias binding – a folded fabric strip, cut on the bias, for encasing raw seam edges

Blind hemming – a small hemming stitch that is virtually invisible from the right side

Bobbin – the spool or reel holding the lower thread for a sewing machine; the bobbin thread combines with the top thread to form stitches and shows on the underside

Bodice – the part of the garment that covers the torso

Boning – thin nylon, plastic or metal strips used to stiffen and shape close-fitting garments such as bodices

Border print – pattern printed along an edge of the fabric, for example Sari fabric

Border print – pattern printed along an edge of the fabric, for example Sari fabric

Box pleats – two symmetrical pleats folded away from each other to leave a flat panel in the centre

Bust point – marked on a commercial pattern, this is where the wearer's fullest bust point should fall

Capped sleeve – a very short sleeve that sits across the top of the arm and shoulder

Casing – the tunnel through which elastic or drawstring is fed and pulled up

Clapper – a wooden pressing aid with different angled sides, used to help press tailored garments

Clipping – a method of reducing bulk in seam allowances by snipping diagonally into the seam allowance close to stitching; used on inner curved seams

Collar stand – found on a tailored shirt, the stand attaches to the neck edge and the collar to provide a vertical lift before the collar falls smoothly back over the neckline

Crosswise grain – formed by weft threads and runs across the width of the fabric, at 90 degrees to the lengthwise grain

Cutting line – the outer line on a commercial pattern piece (a seam line is usually ⅝in (1.5m) inside the cutting line to provide a seam allowance)

Dart – a wedge-shaped section of fabric, folded with the widest part at the garment edge, tapering to nothing; used at the bust, waist and back to help shape a garment to body contours

Dolman sleeves – cut in a single piece with the front or back garment, without a separate sleeve sectionm but with a seam down the centre from shoulder to sleeve hem

Double hem – hem allowance folded in two equal amounts (a 2in (5cm) double hem takes 4in (10cm) of hem allowance); ensures the raw edge is tucked inside and the hem area is evenly thick

Ease – excess fabric in a garment; wearing ease allows for movement; designer ease gives style and shape

Ease stitch – a slightly longer than regular stitch length used to pull up stitching slightly to ease a longer piece of fabric into a slightly shorter one; often used to set sleeves into an armhole

Edge stitching – top stitching close, usually ⅛in (3 mm), to the edge of a garment, to help keep facings from rolling to the front

Entredeux ('between two') – either a lacy trim, used to join two fabric pieces, or a stitch, formed by a wing needle, that leaves holes

Facing – a section added to openings such as neckline or armholes, used to neaten and hide raw edges and provide a clean line

Feed dogs – jagged protrusions that come up through the throat plate on a sewing machine and move backwards and forwards to help feed fabric through as it is stitched

Fibre – the plant or synthetic substance from which a fabric is woven

Finish – the surface treatment on a fabric, usually added after the fabric is woven

Fix stitch (lock stitch) – small stitches taken on the spot to anchor the seam ends

Flat fell seam – stitched and neatened on both sides; used on sportswear and reversible garments

Fold line – shown on paper patterns, this indicates that the tissue pieces need to be placed on the fold of the fabric, so that two symmetrical halves are cut at once

Free motion stitching – term used when feed dogs are dropped and the operator controls the movement of the fabric to determine the size and position of stitches

French curve – a tool used to create smooth curves in pattern design

French seam – seam with encased raw edges

Frog fastening – (see Rouleau loop)

Godet – fabric insert, usually triangular, added to increase the swing and fullness of a skirt or dress; the more godets added, the wider the hemline

Gored – a shaped pattern piece, used for skirts and dresses that is wider at the hem than the waist to provide a fuller hemline and shaped skirt

Grading – a method of reducing bulk in the seam allowance by cutting each allowance to different widths

Grain line – formed by warp fibres, the lengthwise straight grain of the fabric

Gusset – a piece of fabric sewn into

a seam, such as underarm, to provide extra fullness

Hand, handle – term used to describe how a fabric handles, drapes, folds and creases

Hem allowance – fabric that is turned up to form a hem

Hem gauge – a tool with measurements and a slide notch used to mark hem allowances

High bust – measurement taken above the full bust, under the arms and straight across the back, used to determine pattern size when bust size is larger than C cup

Hip point – the widest part of the hips, usually 7–9in (18–23cm) below the waist

Hong Kong seam – seam allowances wrapped with bias binding to conceal and protect the raw edges

Interfacing – a layer of fabric or purpose-made fabric that adds strength and support at specific areas such as collars, cuffs and front facings

Interlining – a second layer of fabric attached to give extra body and warmth to the main fabric

Inverted pleats – two pleats folded towards each other, meeting in the centre, with an inlay of contrasting or self-fabric beneath

Kimono (dolman) sleeves – cut as an extension of the bodice, they can be loose or close fitting

Knife-edge (straight) pleat – pleats formed facing the same direction

Ladder stitch – a method of stitching an opening left for turning out closed

Lapped seam – in which the seam allowances are overlapped and stitched

in place; useful for bulky fabrics that do not fray

Lining – usually lightweight, this is an additional fabric layer adds weight and richness

Lock stitch/locking in – catching a tiny amount of one fabric to another using a single matching thread

Mandarin (Chinese) collar – a short, unfolded stand-up collar that starts at the neckline and stands vertically

Mitre – a neat finish to hemmed corners

Nap – term used to describe the pile of a fabric with surface texture, such as velvet or fur, which causes shading; use 'with nap' layout so all pattern pieces are laid out in the same direction

Notch – triangular mark on the cutting line of a commercial pattern, used to determine how pieces join together; cut around the outer edge of notch when cutting out fabric

Notching – a method of reducing bulk on outer curved seams; cut wedges from the seam allowance so it will lie flat

Notions – haberdashery

Open-ended (separating) zipper – a zipper that comes apart completely so that a garment such as a jacket can be opened

Overlocker/serger – a machine that cuts a seam allowance, sews a seam and overstitches edges together in one pass

Pattern – the design woven into or printed on a fabric; OR a paper template used to determine the shapes and sizes of garment pieces

Pattern layout – diagrams used to show how pattern pieces should be laid onto the fabric

Pattern match – the technique of matching patterns on edges/seams; cut first piece on a single layer of fabric; lay cut piece on the remaining fabric so that next section can be placed to match the pattern at key points; when cutting two of same pattern piece, place the second face down to ensure a left and right

Pattern repeat – measured from the top of the pattern to the top of the next identical pattern

Peplum – a flared 'skirt' attached to the waist of a jacket or top to create a fuller hemline

Pile – surface texture on fabric such as velvet, which stands proud of the fabric base and creates shading; use 'with nap' layout

Pilling (bobbling) – the term used to describe the tiny fabric balls that form on a fabric surface after repeated wear; they can be removed with a fabric shaver; the better the quality of fabric, the less it will pill

Pin tucks – very narrow tucks of fabric stitched in place

Piping (welting) – a separate raised edging to define a outline; made of cord covered with contrast or matching fabric, or a ready-made decorative cord with flange

Pivot – term used to turn fabric without moving from the seam line by leaving the needle down in the fabric, raising the presser foot and turning the work before lowering the presser foot to continue

Placket – an additional section of fabric added to openings such as necks, sleeve or cuff; part of the placket is folded to the outside of the garment

Plastron – interfacing or tailor's canvas that fills the hollow between shoulders and bust; the shape varies depending on the bust size

Pleat – fabric folded concertina fashion to add decorative detail or control fullness (see also Box, Inverted and Knife-edge pleat)

Pleat depth – the total amount of fabric in a pleat from placement line to fold line

Point turner – a small ruler with an angled point used to push out corners; usually includes measurements to use as a hem gauge

Pre-shrinking – it is advisable to wash (to take out any treatments) and possibly shrink some fabrics before starting a dressmaking project

Pressing cloth – a cloth placed between the hot iron and the garment when ironing to provide protection, prevent unwanted shine, and allow pressing at higher temperatures; organza is ideal as it withstands high temperatures and is transparent

Pressing ham – a ham-shaped cushion used to support fabric and press it in the right shape when ironing curves, darts, etc

Prick stitch – a version of back stitch, this is used to hand stitch fine or pile fabrics where machine stitching might spoil the texture: bring the needle up from wrong side, take it back to the wrong side 2–3 fabric threads behind the first needle position, before coming up again about ¼in (6mm) in front

Princess seaming – a seam joining two different-shaped edges, which when stitched together shape the garment; usually start at mid-shoulder or armhole

Raglan sleeves – sleeves with angled sleeve head, starting at the shoulder or neck edge and angled to the side, rather than set into an armhole

Raw edge – the edge of fabric that has not been neatened or finished

Reinforce stitching – used to strengthen areas of a garment that may come under stress, by stitching over the seam line in that area a second time

Rever collar – flat V-shaped collar often found on blouses

Rolled collar – this type of collar is softly rolled where it folds down from the stand, rather than having a pressed crease

Rolled hem – a very narrow hem finish, folded under by ⅛in (3mm), stitched, folded under again along the stitching and stitched again

Rotary cutter – a cutting tool ideal for cutting long straight lengths of fabric

Rouleau loop (frog fastening) – a narrow fabric tube that forms a loop to fasten a round button

Ruffle – a separate length of fabric gathered and attached to a straight edge of another fabric section

Running stitch – a hand stitch used to hold layers of fabric together, made by running the needle from back to front at regular intervals

Satin stitch – a very close machine zigzag stitch; the less the stitch width, the closer the stitches are together

Seam allowance – usually ⅝in (1.5cm) in dressmaking, this is the area between the outer edge and the seam line, which ensures that fabric edges can be neatened and the seams will not fray away off the edge

Seam line – the line on which a seam is stitched when putting two or more fabric pieces together

Seam ripper (quick un-pick) – a tool with a curved blade used to cut open or unpick seams and open buttonholes

Self-covered button – a purpose-made metal or plastic button that can be covered with fabric to match or contrast a garment

Selvage (selvedge) – the bound side edges of a length of fabric that run parallel to the grainline

Set-in sleeves – sleeves that are designed to be fitted into an armhole

Sew-through button – a flat button with two or four holes through which you stitch to sew the button to the garment

Shank button – a button with a loop on the underside that provides a space between the garment and button; used on bulkier garments as the shank allows the fabric to pass through the buttonhole and lay flat beneath

Sheers – transparent fabrics

Sleeve head – the top part of the sleeve, which is attached to the shoulder seam

Slip stitch – a small stitch used to hem lightweight fabrics by picking up only one or two fibres from the main fabric

Spool (spindle) – the thread holder on a sewing machine

Stabilizer – layer of specialist fabric used to prevent fabric from puckering or distorting when stitching; various types are available from tear-away to soluble and iron on

Staystitching – a line of stitching, formed just within the seam allowance close to the seam line, to prevent unwanted stretch when handling the garment pieces

Stitch-in-the-ditch – a row of stitching worked from the right side of the fabric, formed within the seam of previous stitching, used to hold facings, etc. in place

Tacking – (see Basting)

Tailor's tack – a way of hand stitching placement points on garments for buttonholes, darts, pockets, etc.; use a double length of contrasting thread to make two or three very loose loopy stitches through the tissue pattern and both fabric layers; snip into the loops and gently pull the fabric apart, snipping the thread between the layers so that some thread remains in both fabric pieces

Tension (gauge) – tautness of the stitch which comes from the pressure being exerted between the needle and bobbin; on a sewing machine there are two types of tension – thread and bobbin; adjust a little at a time

Toile – a garment made from cheap fabric such as calico to test a pattern and to make sure the garment fits perfectly, essential when using expensive or delicate fabrics on which alterations would mark

Top stitching – stitching that is visible on the surface

Tracing wheel – a little serrated wheel, which, when rolled over the carbon paper, transfers colour to the fabric to mark placement lines for darts, pleats, etc.

Tucks – similar to pin tucks but slightly wider, these folds in fabric are stitched down the full length

Turn of the cloth – the amount of fabric (especially bulkier ones) that is taken up when folding fabric over or turning it to the right side, which must be taken into account when making self-fabric facings on jackets or calculating hem allowances

Underlining – an additional layer of fabric that adds opacity to transparent fabrics, or weight and stability; cut the same size and from the same pattern pieces as main garment sections, and treated as one with the main fabric in the garment construction

Understitching – a row of stitching through seam allowances and facings only, very close to the seam that attaches a facing to the main garment; used to stop the lining or facings from rolling out

Wadding – (see Batting)

Walking foot – a specialist presser foot that has feed dogs to help guide thick layers of fabric through the sewing machine to ensure neat and even seams

Warp – the vertical threads running down the length of the cloth, which were lifted and lowered during weaving

Weft – the woven horizontal threads placed under or over the warp during weaving

Welt – the visible part of the binding on a buttonhole or pocket opening

Welt and double welt seams – seams with top stitching and suitable for heavyweight fabrics; a welt seam has one row of top stitching, a double welt seam two

Welting – (see Piping)

Zigzag stitch – a sideways stitch that moves from left to right

SUPPLIERS

Simplicity Creative Group
PO Box 367, Coronation Street
Stockport
UK
SK5 7WZ
T: + 44 (0) 161 480 6122
E: uk.eusales@simplicity.com
W: www.simplicitynewlook.com

Simplicity Patterns Co Inc
2 Park Avenue
New York
New York, 10016
T: 1-888 588 2700
E: info@simplicity.com
W: www.simplicity.com

Stone Fabrics and Sewing Surgery
97 High Street
Totnes
Devon
TQ9 5PB
T: 01803 868608
E: stone_fabrics@mac.com

Pattern websites

butterick.mccall.com
craftysewer.com
decadesofstyle.com – retro patterns
ethnicpatterns.com
habithat.co.uk
hotpatterns.com – new range of patterns
kwiksew.com / kwiksew.co.uk
mccall.com – McCalls, Butterick and Vogue
Patterns (US site)
patternstop.com
patternsoftime.com – historical
costume patterns
retrofitpattern.com
sewdirect.com – McCalls, Butterick and
Vogue Patterns (UK site)
sewingpatterns.com
simplicitynewlook.com (UK site)
simplicity.com (US site)
venacavadesign.co.uk – patterns and
materials for corset making
vintagefabricmarket.co.uk – vintage patterns
voguepatterns.mccall.com
yourpersonalfit.com

Fabric websites

Abakhan-onlineshop.co.uk – dress and
dance fabrics
Calicolaine.co.uk – bridal and dancewear
fabrics, extensive trims
chrisanne.com – dancewear, fabrics
and trimmings
dalstonmillfabrics.co.uk – specializes in
bridal and dance fabrics
denholme-velvets.co.uk – specialists
in velvet
dotsnstripes.co.uk – continental and
children's fabrics and patterns
dreamyfabrics.co.uk – extensive range,
including eco fabrics

efabrics.co.uk – Chawlas fabric and
haberdashery on line
englishcouture.co.uk – hard-to-find lingerie
fabrics, speed tailoring interfacings, DVDs
e.g. on tailoring/bra making
ericas.com – unusual fabrics, free projects,
gadgets, gizmos, kits and books
fabricuk.com – unusual fabrics
fabricland.co.uk
fabrics4you.co.uk
fabricaz.co.uk – costume fabrics
fabrix.org.uk
fleecylady.com – fleece fabrics with themes
gonetoearth.co.uk – vintage style craft
fabrics, brushed cottons and haberdashery
gorgeousfabrics.com – diverse range
greenfibres.com – organic fabrics
hempfabric.co.uk – eco-friendly, sustainable
fabrics in creamy natural shades
mrosenbergandson.co.uk – great fabrics all
low prices
millcrofttextiles.co.uk
nevtex.co.uk – dancewear fabrics, trims
and haberdashery
oakshottfabrics.com – handloom fabrics
remnanthouse.co.uk – fabric remnants,
including dressmaking and novelty
reprodepotfabrics.com – retro fabrics, trims,
appliqués, haberdashery, patterns
sewing-box.co.uk – fabrics, haberdashery,
sewing boxes, trimmings
sewingchest.co.uk – materials and
haberdashery for bras, corsets, lingerie,
period costumes
sherwoodsfabrics.co.uk – mixed range
of fabrics
thaisilks.com
totallyfabrics.co.uk – fashion fabrics, stretch
and fancy fabrics for dancewear
or costumes

trimfabric.com
twinfabrics.com – great for fleece
vintagefabricmarket.co.uk – vintage fabrics,
patterns, haberdashery, books
vivalafrida.co.uk – Mexican oilcloth fabrics
wolfintextiles.co.uk – linen and
natural cottons

Haberdashery/miscellaneous websites

bridalcoveredbuttons.co.uk – bridal buttons,
eyelets, rouleau loops, boleros
dreamsilk.co.uk – So N Sews website,
specializing in haberdashery
eastmanstaples.co.uk/sew2go/ –
habadashery, pattern paper, grading rulers,
curved rulers
ericas.com – unusual fabrics, free projects,
gadgets, gizmos, kits, books
Harlequin-uk.com – fabric covering service
for trimmings, haberdashery, belts, buttons
Jaycotts.co.uk – assorted haberdashery,
fabric, sewing machines/feet
Kleins.co.uk – haberdashery
sewingmachine-sales.co.uk – zippers of all
kinds, sewing machines, accessories
sewing-online.com – haberdashery, trims
schoolofsewing.co.uk – lingerie fabrics, bra
power nets, bra fittings, accessories
zipperstop.com – zippers of all sorts

Sewing machine websites

bernina.co.uk
bredons.co.uk – Brother, Bernina, HV, Pfaff
plus Babylock overlockers and embellishers,
Elna presses
brother.co.uk / brother.com
direct-sewingmachines.co.uk – Janome,
Bernina and Frister Rossmann, plus one-2-
one courses

gursewingmachines.com – most major brands, free postage, online store
husqvarnaviking.com
janome.co.uk / janome.com
pfaff.com
psmc.co.uk – Pemberton Sewing Machines, sewing machines, feet, fabric, advice
stocks.co.uk – Brother PR620 and Janome MB4 (semi-industrial embroidery machines), advice on running home business
superstitch.co.uk – range of machines, accessories, advice
thesewingstudio.co.uk – multi-brand sewing machine online outlet, good buying advice

Sewing advice websites
isew.co.uk – general sewing techniques, tips, free projects
patternreview.com – US site of pattern reviews, sewing machine reviews and tips, posted by public sewconfused.co.uk – bridalwear advice, leaflets, supplies
sewing.org – US site for Sewing and Craft Alliance, free projects, techniques

ACKNOWLEDGMENTS

With thanks to Dawn Cloake of the Fashion Academy for making all the garments. Thanks also go to Simplicity Creative Group for the lovely patterns and to Stone Fabrics and Sewing Surgery for the fabrics. Finally thanks to my family – Lez, Jake and Charlie – for their forbearance while I write and sew!

ABOUT THE AUTHOR

Wendy Gardiner has been influential in the sewing industry for many years and is an internationally accredited sewing guru. She is currently Editor of *Sewing World magazine*, author of a number of sewing books, and writer and presenter of several sewing DVDs. Wendy strongly believes in sharing sewing skills and knowledge so that more people can make their own fashion and furnishings, and realize that these projects can be fast, fun and simple to create. Among the many sewing and craft books she has written, the most recent titles include *The Sewing Bible Curtains* and *The Sewing Bible Slipcovers*. Her latest DVDs include *Sew Easy Dressmaking 2 and 3*, follow-ons from *Dressmaking that's Fast and Fun*, *Sew Easy Creative Customising* and *Sew Easy Special Fabrics*. Wendy is passionate about encouraging people to have a go and sew!

INDEX